The Lockert Library of Poetry in Translation

ADVISORY EDITOR: DARYL HINE

For other titles in the Lockert Library see page 278.

The Silence Afterwards

Selected Poems of Rolf Jacobsen

TRANSLATED AND EDITED
BY ROGER GREENWALD

FOREWORD BY POUL BORUM

❄   ❄   ❄   ❄   ❄

Princeton University Press
Princeton, New Jersey

Norwegian poems © 1982 by Gyldendal Norsk Forlag A/S
English translations and Introduction © 1985 by Roger Greenwald
Foreword © 1985 by Poul Borum
Published by Princeton University Press, 41 William Street,
Princeton, New Jersey 08540
In the United Kingdom: Princeton University Press, Guildford, Surrey

ISBN 0-691-06647-7
ISBN 0-691-01424-8 (pbk.)

The Lockert Library of Poetry is supported by a bequest from
Charles Lacy Lockert (1888-1974)

The translator is grateful to the Translation Center at Columbia
University for a Translation Center Award received in 1983

Translation of this book has been aided by the Norwegian Cultural
Council and by the Norsemen's Federation

Some of these translations have appeared in WRIT, *Translation, Stand,
The Spirit That Moves Us, Scandinavian Review, Rubicon, Poetry East,
The Norseman* (Oslo), and *Nordisk Tidende* (Brooklyn)

This book has been composed in Linotron Granjon
Clothbound editions of Princeton University Press books are printed
on acid-free paper, and binding materials are chosen for strength and
durability. Paperbacks, although satisfactory for personal collections,
are not usually suitable for library rebinding

Printed in the United States of America by Princeton University Press,
Princeton, New Jersey

Translator's dedication: For Luigi M. Bianchi

Contents

vii

xi

Foreword

Rolf Jacobsen as a European Poet

ROLF JACOBSEN is not well known to English-speaking readers, so the first thing to do is to place him in time and space. Biographically it is easy: Norwegian, born 1907 and still alive, has spent most of his life as a journalist at a provincial newspaper; he published his first two books of poetry in 1933 and 1935, then had a comeback in 1951, and has since published eight more books, the latest in 1979. He and his contemporary Olav H. Hauge are now regarded as the old masters among living Norwegian poets.

Jacobsen's first two books went unnoticed; they were too "strange," too modernistic both in themes (technology) and in form (free verse) to have any impact on the conservative literary milieu in Norway, and it was only when a new generation of poets in the 1960s needed predecessors that Jacobsen was "found." The new Jacobsen who emerges in the books published since 1951 can in no way be called an extreme modernist. He is not in any sense a "literary" poet, and it is futile to look for influences, local or international. But there is no doubt that the slowly changing literary climate in Norway in the forties and fifties sustained his comeback, and he has not only been a teacher for new generations of poets, but has also learned from them.

In an international context, Jacobsen belongs to a generation of poets, most of them born in the first decade of the century, who published their first books in the thirties: Auden and Empson in England, George Oppen and the other Williams pupils in America—"objectivism" is also a key word for understanding Jacobsen—Drummond de Andrade in Brazil and Gabriel Celaya in Spain, Pavese in Italy, Milosz in Poland, Guillevic in France, Günther Eich and Ernst Meister in Germany, Gunnar Ekelöf and Harry Martinson in Sweden. Apart from Ekelöf, who developed into one of the greatest and most original poets of the century, most of these poets are less spectacular than the great generation of modernists born in the 1880s and nineties. They are marked by the economic and political detour of the thirties, and the general reticence of their style can be seen as a reaction to the literary boom of Isms in the twenties: they did not *want* to be spectacular.

Like many novelists of the thirties, these poets tend toward greater "realism," including a direct "social consciousness" for which there was no room in the metaphorical orgies of the surrealists. To place Rolf Jacobsen in perspective, it is useful to see him in connection with William Carlos Williams and D. H. Lawrence, but also with Brecht and Francis Ponge. The worship of things, of the "thinginess" of this world, he has in common with both Williams and Ponge, and his cosmic sensuality is Laurentian, while his calm irony is often like Brecht's, what Brecht called "cunning."

This realistic trend in modern poetry, co-existing with the more "lofty" poetry, is metonymic in Roman Jakobson's sense as against metaphorical, but it must be remembered that Jakobson insisted that both modes of expression are always present in the same poet. Rolf Jacobsen and many of the other poets of the thirties developed, and one can see their development as the finding of individual solutions to "the problem of metaphor."

I am sure that Jacobsen's daily journalistic practice has been the greatest influence on his poetry. (Of course his poems are not "journalistic" in a bad, superficial sense.) The conciseness of good journalism seems to have taught him to develop one important metaphor through a poem. And his feeling for the essential has allowed him to create myths out of his commitment to the everyday world (including its historical and astronomical past).

In its quiet insistence on fundamental qualities of life, the poetry of Rolf Jacobsen is unique and at the same time deeply connected to a consciously humanistic trend in European modernism.

Poul Borum

Introduction

Rolf Jacobsen's Poetry

ROLF JACOBSEN'S POETRY is special for two reasons: because it opened a new chapter in Norwegian poetry, and because it explores life with a distinctive sensibility and voice. Rolf Jacobsen was born on 8 March 1907. He grew up in Oslo, but has lived most of his life in the smaller city of Hamar, about 60 miles (95 km) north of Oslo, on the eastern shore of Lake Mjøsa. He has made his living as a journalist.

In 1933, when Jacobsen published his first book, most poetry in Norway was still written in traditional meters, and most of it was rhymed. It drew its images from traditional sources—myth, nature, religion, seafaring, and warfare—and almost always, it maintained an elevated, "poetic" tone.

Jacobsen's first book broke new ground: many of the poems were in unrhymed free verse, and used diction and vocabulary close to those of speech; and many treated subjects or used images drawn from the modern industrial city. Of course Jacobsen had some forerunners in Norway. Several poets of stature departed from standard meters on occasion, and the proletarian writer Kristofer Uppdal (1878-1961) made use of unvarnished details from urban and industrial life. But Jacobsen is now widely recognized as the poet who launched modernism in his country (the poet Claes Gill [1910-1973] made an important contribution a few years later). It is not necessary to conduct a detailed analysis to convince oneself how far Jacobsen had come. Notwithstanding the connecting threads that can always be traced from one period to the next, anyone who reads aloud a few lyrics by Bjørnson (1832-1910) and a few by Jacobsen will hear the nineteenth century in one ear and the twentieth in the other.[1]

The change to what we now regard as modern subjects and

---

[1] An examination of the ways in which Jacobsen's choice of words enriched and renewed poetic vocabulary in Norwegian lies beyond the scope of this introduction, and also beyond my area of competence.

styles was slow in coming to Norway. The new age had already arrived in the poetry of several other countries. But Jacobsen's poems in the modern style are not mere imitations of imported models; poems like "Reise" ("Travel") and "Byens metafysikk" ("Metaphysics of the City") show that he had made a new way of looking and writing his own.

Yet in *Jord og jern* (Earth and Iron), as the title suggests, Jacobsen took care to forge a connection between the old and the new. The titles in the book's first section indicate subjects drawn from nature; almost all of these poems are in unrhymed free verse. It is as if Jacobsen drew his readers into his new style with themes he knew they would be comfortable with. The titles in the third section bring us unambiguously into the modern world; yet here Jacobsen does not hesitate, in treating urban themes, to use rhyme or fairly regular meter occasionally when they suit his purposes.

Because Jacobsen seemed at first to be a champion of technological progress, member of a generation that could find poetry in machines, much has been written about his supposed change from an admirer to a skeptic or outright critic of technology. But even in his first two books he distinguishes between beneficial and oppressive aspects of the modern scene, and often finds each aspect implied in the other. In "Dirrende telefonstolper" ("Vibrating Telephone Poles"), for example, the message is mixed: the poles as antennae listening to outer space are at first presented as wonderful; the signals they pick up are described, by the end of the poem, with horrifying images. In treating technologies, Jacobsen always focuses on the relation they have to what is human, or on the light that their use as metaphors can cast on what is human. That is why air travel, subways, television, and advertising earn harsh treatment, newspapers and radio get better than even breaks, and railroads inspire lifelong admiration.

It will repay the reader to trace the railroad as it winds its way through Jacobsen's books. On the historical plane (which has become steadily more important in relation to many subjects as Jacobsen's work has matured), the English-speaking reader needs to know that the building of Norway's railroads in the last half of the nineteenth century and the beginning of the twentieth not only bound together some of the distant and isolated parts of a country that extends for over 1,000 miles (1,700 km), but represented a feat of railway engineering unrivaled anywhere. The *rallare* (navvies) who built the railroads still have, for many Norwegians, the status of folk heroes. Moreover, the Norwegian railroad, as a state-owned enterprise, can be felt by ordinary Norwegian citizens to be in some sense "theirs."

The subject seems inexhaustible for Jacobsen, and his meditations on it have increased in complexity. "Jernbaneland" ("Railroad Country"), in his first book, suggests how rich the subject is for the poet at the beginning of his career. The poem's last section, a sort of industrial Call of the Wild that bears a strong flavor of the thirties, has obvious sexual undertones, and makes plain the speaker's ambivalence about what is freedom, what escapism. Eleven books later, in "Inlandsbanan" ("The Inland Line"), we find the poet riding past abandoned towns on a decaying Swedish line built long ago, at high human cost, to transport soldiers and their weapons. As if that weren't bad enough, at the end of the poem the whole bewildering modern world intrudes by way of newspapers brought aboard for sale. Yet even here, amid the sorrow, we pick up in the evoked journey a whiff of something more than nostalgia: the ineradicable scent of travel. For Jacobsen has ridden the trains, lived near them, watched and listened to them, and written some of his best poems about them. How touching for a North American to learn that the Norwegian State Railway returns the favor by giving the poet a pass for a free trip each year!

*

Jacobsen's poetry is, of course, much more than a penetrating commentary on the modern external world, and indeed, this aspect of his work becomes less important, though no less evident, as soon as one turns to his third and fourth books, *Fjerntog*

(Express Train) and *Hemmelig liv* (Secret Life). Here the poems seem to come from a greater depth: they emerge from contemplation (not without humor); they deal with eternal themes as well as with the current condition; and they begin to show a conscious use of history. Poems like "Solsikke" ("Sunflower"), "På Varaldskogen" ("In the Varald Forest"), "Tømmer" ("Timber"), "Alderdommen" ("Old Age"), "Turnipshøst" ("Turnip Crop"), "Sorgfulle tårn" ("Mournful Towers") and "Stavkirker" ("Stave Churches") force us to consider what is fundamental to the way Jacobsen has written ever since.

Jacobsen's writing combines an ancient way of looking—a way that searches for connectedness—with an openness to the new, even to things that reveal no connectedness and would resist attempts to impose it. In other words, Jacobsen has a strong sense of the world as mystery, and he approaches that mystery with reverence. His sensibility is a religious one—not much concerned with doctrine, but very much concerned with spirit, with the preciousness of life, with unity, and with the exertions necessary to receive ever fresh manifestations of these qualities. It is not important whether we mean "receive" literally or as a metaphor for a certain type of experience. What is important is that even in his less successful poems, Jacobsen can never be accused of opportunism toward his subjects. His world is not fodder for technique. It may be that Jacobsen receives certain types of meaning more readily and more clearly than others, but that does not mean he is trying to subsume the whole world in one Procrustean song. His is a spirit that is receptive and contemplative, yet does not need to deny or divest itself of personality in the Western sense. All that is required is a measure of humility.

The way Jacobsen writes evinces his humility at every turn. In the first place, he has tried to create poems that will be accessible, though not oversimplified. Second, he concentrates on subjects other than the self, treating himself mainly as an instrument for their elucidation. Where the voice is powerful and heavily stressed, as in "Sorgfulle tårn" ("Mournful Towers") or "Stenhistorien" ("The History of Stone"), the forcefulness comes to inhere in the subject; it does not insist on itself as a quality of the speaker's. Even the poems that refer to themselves often declare that the natural world acts upon them, rather than the other way around. In "Grønt lys" ("Green Light"), for example, the poet says that the winds spread his poems out like dust, and that seeds sprout between the letters in his words.

Jacobsen hardly puts himself forward at all. We learn only a little about his everyday life from his poems, and almost nothing about his personal relations. Jacobsen is concerned to render his experience of his own and his readers' surroundings, and the ideas and feelings that attach to that encounter. His poems do not pay much attention to the occupations of his body or the workings of his unconscious. They are more closely aligned to the seasons of the earth than to the inclinations of the ego.

The importance of nature in Jacobsen's work is obvious, and places him in a long tradition of Norwegian writing. The rivers, mountains, trees, stones, and skies of Norway serve as settings, as characters, and as sources of metaphor. Jacobsen is interested in people's relation to the natural world, their relation to the man-made world, and the ways in which these two relations affect each other. His sensitivity to nature, and the access to self that it grants him, inform both his enthusiasms and his regrets about our culture.

English-speaking readers need to keep a few things in mind if they are to grasp this dimension of Jacobsen's poetry. First, we sometimes need to ask ourselves what is happening. Poems like "Nu bærer elven sine lamper ut" ("Now the River Is Carrying Off Its Lights") or "Fossestøperen" ("The Foundryman of Waterfalls"), for example, will make immediate sense to Norwegian readers, but may seem mysterious to us unless we realize, in one case, that the time is summer and the streams are drying up, and in the other, that waterfalls in forests make certain kinds of sounds.

Second, we need to realize that although the ways in which

Jacobsen treats nature can be analyzed and his attitudes toward it studied in relation to those of various literary traditions, it would be a mistake to regard the pervasiveness of nature in his work as the product mainly of one or another literary stance. Nature is a powerful presence in Norway, and few Norwegians grow up without a strong sense of that presence. Jacobsen, like any Norwegian poet who decides to speak of nature at all, is dealing with an everyday fact of life, a form and a force with which he is on intimate terms.

A mountain has one kind of effect on people who are looking at it as tourists, with urban shapes and scales in their heads, and another kind of effect on people who have walked its paths and climbed its rocks year in and year out. Once again, we see that Jacobsen's surroundings are not "material" for poems, but almost internalized parts of the speaker. The result is an unusual quality—perhaps shared by some Chinese and Japanese writing. The poet does not enter the rock; the rock has entered the poet, and the poet takes account of that when he speaks.

*

What, then, is the method that Jacobsen has developed to embody his mode of seeing and listening? Taking his cue from a poem in *Headlines*, the Danish poet and critic Poul Borum writes that Jacobsen attempts,

> through imaginative perception, to create a balance be-
> tween metaphor and myth, that is, between transforma-
> tion and unity. His fundamental experience of the world
> (people, nature, culture) is transforming, is a paraphras-
> ing in images, a saying that this is like something else,
> but the core is tremblingly static, is myth. That this
> myth is empty is a basic condition in modernism and in
> the twentieth century. The emptiness, seen negatively, is
> the stagnation in the midst of transformation — Rolf
> Jacobsen's fear of the transitional states of morning and
> evening; experienced positively, it is stillness, the inner-
> most mystic silence—his cultivation of the unity day-

and-night. Anxiety is mastered with the imagination's precision, and the eternal is discovered in the eternally fleeting.[2]

Silence lies at the core of Jacobsen's work in more senses than one. That he often takes it as his subject is obvious from titles like "Stillheten i trær" ("The Silence in Trees") and "Stillheten efterpå" ("The Silence Afterwards"). Jacobsen's use of images, by powerfully evoking the visual and often by setting two pictures side by side, moves the reader beyond the words and into a "silent" realm. Despite marked differences in style, one could say that Jacobsen's work anticipates a quality Ted Hughes has noted among poets of Eastern Europe in the next generation (Vasko Popa, Miroslav Holub, Zbigniew Herbert): that they aim at "making audible meaning without disturbing the silence."[3] Certainly Jacobsen is a poet with a profound respect both for the silence that precedes and follows his acts of speech and for the silence that inheres in things: their unnamable qualities, which the writer must respect if his efforts are to yield up some sense of them.

Jacobsen's practice of presenting not only plants and animals but inanimate objects as if they were endowed with human capacities of observation and feeling reflects his effort to discover unspoken truths about his surroundings and about us. Seen from outside, this practice can be called simply "personification"; and indeed, when the poems fail, the method can seem to be little more than a device. But when the poems succeed, they capture a strange and delicate quality, and sometimes give us the eerie sensation that we are being regarded; so it is clear that Jacobsen has arrived at the heart of his subject. That success cannot be the result of the mechanical application of a device. An observation by Walter Benjamin provides a useful way of thinking

[2] Borum, "Rolf Jacobsen's hemmelige sprog," *Minerva's Kvartalskrift*, 1 (1970), p. 37 (my translation).
[3] "Introduction," in Vasko Popa, *Collected Poems*, trans. Anne Pennington (New York: Persea, 1978), p. 3.

about the process and the impulse that lies behind it: "To perceive the aura of an object, we look at means to invest it with the ability to look at us in return."[4]

In Poul Borum's elegant description, Jacobsen's

> double task has been to give his lightness weight and his gravity lightness—where the first fails, the poems flutter off without obligations, like paper butterflies of metaphor, and where the second fails, they sink to the ground like unambiguous (satiric or tragic) fragments of myth. The most successful poems in his books could be called *metaphor-myths*; they attain effortlessly the nervous partnership of unity and transformation that is his fundamental experience.[5]

Especially in poems that capture the spirit of place, we can see Jacobsen's search for unity and his respect for silence as two aspects of the same posture. "Avaldsnes," "Bortafor Grorud —" ("Beyond Grorud —"), "Tårnene i Bologna" ("The Towers in Bologna"), "Avignon, Vaucluse," "Småbyer i Auvergne" ("Old Cities in Auvergne"), "Klokkene fra Assisi" ("The Bells from Assisi"), "Silvery Moon"—all these poems evoke not only the particular flavor of the places contemplated, but a hovering presence that gives each place a niche in a larger expanse, just as the place seems to set the human observer (and the reader) in one of its inconspicuous corners, like a tiny figure in a Chinese landscape painting.

*

If we look closely at Jacobsen's poems with a view to understanding how their verbal textures embody his attitudes toward both language and the world, we will notice a quality that the American critic and translator James Larson has aptly called

---

[4] "On Some Motifs in Baudelaire," in *Illuminations*, trans. Harry Zohn (New York: Harcourt, Brace & World, 1968), p. 188.

[5] Borum, p. 37 (my translation).

decorum. It is obvious that Jacobsen's choice of subjects honors, for whatever reason, certain limits drawn around areas that have often been considered unsuitable for public exposure. But Larson is making a point not about subject matter, but about words.

> There is one essential quality uniting [Jacobsen's early and later works], and it has to do with the unfashionable problem of propriety or decorum. Jacobsen's ambition as a poet has always been to present his subjects naively and distinctly, without addition or subtraction. His poetry is clear but not familiar, and simple but never facile; its justice lies almost entirely in the choice and propriety of terms. This is an ambition more praiseworthy than brilliant, and it has served—if not in intention, at least in effect—to limit his audience and to delay recognition.[6]

Larson has pinpointed the principles that govern Jacobsen's poems insofar as they are presentations of subjects (they are also, of course, musical structures of feeling). Poetry written on these principles is not flashy. For Jacobsen, things are things and words are words. He introduces objects into his poems primarily because he wants to say something about them or wants the reader to see them, not because he wants the sound or tone of the words that name them. (Readers who find Jacobsen's use of the definite article as noticeable as I do will perhaps agree that it reflects a deep-seated aspect of his view of his surroundings— a perception of particularity that is childlike, and a conception of archetype that is mythic.) For the most part, Jacobsen is content with the "thingness" of things, and likewise with the "wordness" of words: he does not use words as little visual and sonic objects divorced from meaning. He is masterful in his use of the musical qualities of language, and from time to time plays with words—breaking them up and getting new meaning out of the pieces, or punning, sometimes across dialects—but the

---

[6] Review of *Samlede dikt* (1977), *World Literature Today*, 52 (1978), 479.

music and the play serve integral purposes in the poems, most often the traditional one of conveying the speaker's attitude toward his subjects and his statements.

It begins to sound as though Jacobsen, the pioneering modernist, is conservative. And in a sense, of course, he is, in that he seeks to conserve certain ancient values in life (contemplation, harmony) and in art (meaning, beauty). But we must go even further and recognize what Larson's description implies: that although Jacobsen broke away from established subjects, treatments, and forms, his method nonetheless has a great deal in common with that of classical authors, in that he aims for simplicity, balance, and controlled, though powerful, emotion. If this is a combination that has deprived Jacobsen's work of allure in a given year's marketplace, it is also a synthesis that has yielded lasting value. The honesty of their engagement with their times has always made the poems seem, on publication, to be current; while their controlled yet unstrained style has kept the best of them—and these are many—from becoming dated. In a large number of Jacobsen's poems, ordinary readers and students of literature alike find that combination of freshness and exact fit of music to statement and feeling that bestows a permanent "rightness" on a piece of writing. These poems live in the mind, and we go back to them.

*

To read through Jacobsen's collected poems, or even a generous selection, is to become aware of a few long-term developments and many continuing strands. I have already noted some examples of each; here I would like at least to mention a few more—traits that come into sharpest focus when one looks back over a body of work that spans fifty years.

Within his framework of metaphor and myth, Poul Borum discerns a development in Jacobsen's work "from the first three books' emphasis on oppositions within similarities to the later books' connection of the large and the small."[7] Jacobsen's some-

---

[7] Borum, p. 37 (my translation).

what uncommon interest in effects of scale is certainly evident in many poems from his fourth and later books, for example "Månen og apalen" ("The Moon and the Apple Tree"), "Grønt lys" ("Green Light"), and "Ovenfra, nedenfra og fra siden" ("From Above, from Below and from the Side"). But we can also find such effects, already well developed, in early poems such as "Gummi" ("Rubber") and "Dirrende telefonstolper" ("Vibrating Telephone Poles").

Jacobsen's quest for the spirit of his surroundings often leads him to describe an "other" world behind or beneath the visible one. In reading some of his earlier poems, such as "Speilglass" ("Plate Glass") or "Den omvendte sommeren" ("The Inverted Summer"), we may wonder whether the poet has detected a truth behind appearances or rather too readily fantasized an alternative existence and sailed off into it. The notion that there is "another" world behind the real one, or through the looking glass, crops up so often that it takes on the flavor of an escapist wish, quite aside from any insights it may offer. It becomes a metaphysical analogue of the longing to travel. But when we arrive at "— En annen sol" ("— A Second Sun"), "Nattvindu" ("Night Window"), and "Tankeløs —" ("Unthinking —"), we see that Jacobsen has firm command of this theme and is using it to get at states of mind that might be inaccessible without it.

On balance, the continuities in Jacobsen's work seem far more striking than the shifts. Strands of recurring but finely adjusted imagery, and of repeated words and phrases, not only contribute to the coherence of his individual volumes but show the constancy of Jacobsen's concerns and his willingness to go back for another try. To take a notable example, Jacobsen has made the image of the earth in space vivid and moving again and again— several times, it is worth remarking, before the Apollo missions brought the picture home on film. Sometimes a phrase in one poem clearly refers to another poem so as to comment or expand on the meaning of the first instance. Thus the poet who observes "the river carrying off its lights" in a poem that ends with an intimation of human mortality in general, becomes in his next book a particular person subject to the same process:

"soon the river will carry off my images" ("Langsomt — —"
["Slowly — —"]).

Perhaps the most touching chords we become aware of when
we read Jacobsen's latest work with his previous poems in mind
are the resolutions achieved by poems that take as their explicit
subjects features that have been implicit through many books
and many years. For such poems have the character of sum-
mings-up in which the poet finally steps forward. In "Se opp
(OBS. OBS.)" ("Look Up [N.B. N.B.]"), Jacobsen explains why
he is fond of clouds and gray weather; in "— Mere fjell"
("— More Mountains") why he is content among the timeless
hills. "Vi som bor ved jernbanen" ("We Who Live near the
Railway") is a wonderfully relaxed and personal poem about a
lifelong obsession. The last line of this poem illustrates Jacobsen's
consummate way with the music of place names; yet in the next
book we find the poet outdoing himself in "Hundvåko," a poem
about—place names and what they mean to him. Finally, in
"Uten en lyd" ("Without a Sound"), Jacobsen pronounces on
silence itself:

> What is intense has no voice.
> Whatever means something. Not the dark of night.
> Not the sunlight. Not death.

Luckily for us, Jacobsen dares nonetheless to give voice to an
echo of intensity, an undercurrent of meaning.

Selection and Translation

To select the poems for this book, I read all the poems in the
1982 edition of Rolf Jacobsen's *Samlede dikt* [Collected Poems],
which collects virtually the entire contents of the eleven volumes
published separately from 1933 to 1979. My first criterion was
simply the quality of each poem in my judgment.[8] After trans-

---

[8] After reading the article by Poul Borum that I have cited here, I went
back and reconsidered several poems that he praised and that I either had not

lating a large number of poems, I selected among the translations, this time on the basis of both the quality of the originals and the success of the translations as poems in English.[9] I have not set out to make the selection representative of subjects, styles, or any other features, but I am hopeful that the large number of poems here will give the reader a broad, though perhaps not comprehensive, survey of Jacobsen's range.

My aim in the translations has been to write good poems in English that capture the movement, tone, and to whatever degree possible, some of the texture of the originals as I interpret them, while at the same time remaining faithful to those originals' exact sense, nuances, and—again, wherever possible—ambiguities. In pursuit of this unattainable ideal I have of course tried to avoid the slavish copying of Norwegian constructions, and have searched for equivalent rather than strictly parallel formulations.[10] In a few poems I felt it was essential to mimic Jacobsen's rhyming or rhythms, but I tried to write these pieces to the same standard of naturalness that governed all the others.

I have not considered it my job to "improve" the original poems. I have also tried not to impose my own stylistic preferences on them. I know, however, that I must inevitably have done so to some extent, if for no other reasons than that Jacobsen writes in his language and I in mine, and that Norwegian and English are considerably different despite their proximity on the Germanic branch of the Indo-European tree.

Where I have departed from Jacobsen's punctuation it has usually been to make intelligible in English certain relations that are discernible in Norwegian from different conventions (the

---

translated or had deleted. As a result, I translated and included in the book the poem "Turnipshøst" ("Turnip Crop"), which I might otherwise have overlooked.

[9] At this stage I had the valuable advice of Charles Douglas, and in a later redaction, that of Richard M. Lush.

[10] I wish to record here my debt to one of Robert Bly's translations in *Twenty Poems* (see the bibliography): from his version of "Solsikke" ("Sunflower") I appropriated several words and phrases that seemed happier choices than my own.

common use of commas, for example, where English calls for semicolons) or from different syntax (for example, the inversion of subject and verb that marks, even in the absence of the usual comma, the beginning of an independent clause after a subordinate element). On rare occasions I have departed from Jacobsen's line breaks because differences in the length and weight of English equivalents made it impossible to maintain the line units supported by the Norwegian.

The reader who has no knowledge of Norwegian can do two things that will be of help in getting from the English versions as much of the feel of the originals as I have been lucky enough to invest the translations with. The first is to read *slowly*, and preferably aloud; the second is to make some attempt to approximate the Norwegian pronunciation of proper names.

Poetry in Norwegian usually moves more slowly than poetry in English—in large part because of differences between the sound qualities of the two languages. The frequency of hard consonants, the clustering of consonants, the diphthongs, and the long vowels combine to make Norwegian a language that gives one more to chew on than English does. Moreover, the large number of monosyllables and of compounded nouns frequently produces dense patterns of stresses and half-stresses, especially when a poet decides to write compactly. These two characteristics together can easily produce a caesura in a line of Norwegian poetry where the equivalent English line, even with the same number of stressed and unstressed syllables, would flow without pause.

Since Jacobsen is fond of place names and a master at employing their musical qualities, there is no way around the need to make a stab at pronouncing them with at least the right stress patterns, and if at all possible, with some approximation of their sounds. Since few readers can remember and consistently apply a table of roughly equivalent sounds, I have chosen not to offer a two-page course in tongue-twisting, and to supply instead a phonetic transcription of each name. Most readers who have used American dictionaries will find the system of transcription familiar.

I have tried in the notes to supply the English-speaking reader with about as much information about background and references as a Norwegian reader might be expected to have, including those details about place names that seemed relevant to an understanding of the poems. I have also explained, for the benefit of the reader who has some access to the original, the handful of cases where it might be difficult to see how I have arrived at my English version.

I will be happy if this book leads any readers to learn enough Norwegian so that their newfound appreciation of the language makes them dissatisfied with reading translations.

The Text

The basis for the Norwegian text printed in this book must be considered to be the 1982 edition of Rolf Jacobsen's *Samlede dikt*. This edition collects the eleven volumes published by 1979 and incorporates the poet's latest revisions up to the date of publication. Unfortunately, it is extremely unreliable typographically, and contains errors that are difficult to distinguish from intentional revisions. Typographically, the 1973 Lanterne paperback edition of *Samlede dikt*, which collects nine volumes, is a better text, though it too contains some errors.

The present Norwegian text is the result of two processes. First, I have collated the 1973, 1977, and 1982 editions of *Samlede dikt*, and have compared corrected versions of the texts printed in the 1982 edition with the poems as they appeared in their original volumes. Second, I have engaged in a lengthy correspondence with Rolf Jacobsen about his revisions and about typographical problems, and have adjusted the texts in accordance with his answers. The English translations are based on the Norwegian texts printed en face.

The spelling in the Norwegian texts is almost always that of the original editions of the books from which the poems have been taken, so that changes from book to book reveal changes in Rolf Jacobsen's orthography in the course of his career. In a handful of instances, spellings in original editions have been changed here because they do not accurately reflect Jacobsen's usage at the time of first publication. Proofs of the Norwegian texts in this book have been checked by the author.

Acknowledgments

I would like to thank four people who have helped me substantially to endow my versions with whatever merits they may enjoy. Rolf Jacobsen has been most generous in his encouragement, his trust, and his patience with my questions. Guro Ekeland elucidated the subtleties of the Norwegian texts with unfailing insight. Charles Douglas and Richard M. Lush have spent endless hours pondering my choices; each has given me the benefit of his fine ear for English.

I express my thanks also to several others who helped me along the way: to Luigi Bianchi, Anne Michaels and Poul Borum for reading a draft of the translation and making many valuable suggestions, to Rolf Sagen for sending copies of critical articles, to Ivar Klausen for help with correspondence, to Eva Lie-Nielsen at Gyldendal Norsk Forlag, and to the many people (chief among them Inger Haug) who made helpful comments on particular translations or who put up with my questions about everything from botany to railroad cars.

For kindly taking the time to comment on a draft of the introduction, I am indebted to Paal-Helge Haugen and Knut Ødegård. The shortcomings are mine, not theirs.

R.G.
March 1984

The Silence Afterwards

❊   ❊   ❊   ❊   ❊

fra JORD OG JERN

* * * * *

1933

from EARTH AND IRON

❋   ❋   ❋   ❋   ❋

1933

Myr

Spettet ut over landet ligger de gule myrer
som flekker av pest.

Gråbleke i regnet og med tåkehette brer de sin
tristhet som endeløse hav mellem tynne skoger.

Rødflammet og mosegule ligger de i solskinnet
og slikker himlen med sin tunge
av søt os.

Og noen kranser sig med unge bjerker, som
flokker av lyse piker står de og grer sitt hår
over lyngtuene.

Og noen hyller sig i en krave av brennende
blomster som de lokker til sig ut av
skogene, i en have av mjødurt, storkenebb
og hvit skogstjerne.

Og alle har de denne besettende ånde,
denne bitre lukt av søt vin. Mange mil
gjennem skogen kan jeg kjenne den som
en bedøvelse for min tanke.

4

Marshes

Spotted out over the land the yellow marshes lie
like patches of plague.

Sallow gray in the rain and with cowls of fog they
      spread their
sadness like endless seas among thin forests.

Streaked red and moss-yellow they lie in the sunshine
and lick the sky with their tongue of
sweet odor.

And some garland themselves with young birches, like
groups of fair girls they stand combing their hair
over the clumps of heather.
And some wrap themselves in a collar of flaming
flowers they lure out of
the woods: in a garden of meadowsweet, crane's-bill
and white wintergreen.

And they all have this engrossing breath,
this bitter smell of sweet wine. Many miles
through the forest I can feel it
anesthetizing my thought.

Skyene

Skyene ruller.
Skyene går og kommer
søvngjengerstille ut fra uendeligheten,
belte bak belte
og tog bak tog,
og skifter farve på jorden.

Og noen dager er det koldt — ett sted.
Og noen dager er det varmt — ett sted.
En dal blir rød i øst.
En dal blir blå i vest
så langt den går.

Skyene ruller.
Belte kommer bak belte
og tog bak tog
og skifter farve på jorden.

Og dagen reiser i tunnell, sånn:
— blink, blink, blink.
Og under kikhullene kommer en mann ut og sier:
«Nei for en sommer vi får.»
Og under skyggeflekkene
blir jorden grå som graven.

Skyene ruller.
Skyhavet beveger sig.
Sol-toppet,
skumrevet, hvitt

The Clouds

The clouds roll on.
Silent as sleepwalkers the clouds
keep coming from infinity,
bank behind bank
and line after line,
and change colors on the earth.

And some days it's cold — somewhere.
And some days it's warm — somewhere.
A valley turns red in the east.
A valley turns blue in the west
as far as it reaches.

The clouds roll on.
Bank comes behind bank
and line after line
and changes colors on the earth.

And the day travels in a tunnel, thus:
— blink, blink, blink.
And under the peepholes a man comes out and says:
"My what a summer we'll be getting."
And under the shadow-patches
the earth turns gray as the grave.

The clouds roll on.
The cloud-ocean moves.
Sun-capped,
foam-reefed, white

i lag på lag
og siler lyset på menneskene
og legger ny farve på deres ansikter.

Noen blir røde som blod.
Noen blir gustne som sopp i skogen.
Noen blir hvite som sne
og noen gule som honning.

layer upon layer.
And filters the light onto people
and sets new color on their faces.

Some become red like blood.
Some become pale like mushrooms in the forest.
Some become white like snow
and some yellow like honey.

Reise

Stasjonsventesaler om natten
med den kjølige atmosfære av rå cement
og jern,
med rekker av visnede smørbrød under
glassdiskene,
opstablede stoler i skyggen,
vaskekonenes strøm over perrongene
i den fuktige morgentime,
kan fylle min sjel med villhet.

Reise mot fremmede lande.
Røk gjennem kupévinduene, skinnenes
magiske sanger. — Paris, Marseille.

Når asfalten har krystet mine føtter
til glør,
når butikkvinduenes glitrende øine
har mistet sin trolldom
og min verden står stille og bare
stirrer på mig,
da går jeg ofte til jernbanestasjonene
hvor de hvite røksøiler setter glade
spørsmålstegn på himlen,
eller til havnen
hvor de store skib ligger med duft av
maling og hav og skinner av lys.

Jeg vil ride på stavnen av et slikt skib
inn mot en ny by.

Jeg vil høre på bølgene pusle om skrogets plater
når vi glir med sakte fart inn mot de

Travel

Station waiting-rooms at night
with the cool atmosphere of raw cement
and iron,
with rows of wilted sandwiches under
glass counters,
stacked-up chairs in the shadows,
runnels across the platforms from charwomen's mops
in the damp morning hour,
can fill my soul with wildness.

Travel to foreign lands.
Smoke through compartment windows, the magic
song of the rails. — Paris, Marseilles.

When the asphalt has turned my feet
into live coals,
when the shop windows' glittering eyes
have lost their spell
and my world stands still and just
stares at me,
then I often go to the railway stations,
where the white columns of smoke set lively
question marks in the sky,
or to the harbor,
where the great ships lie with a fragrance of
paint and ocean, shining with lights.

I want to ride on the bow of such a ship
in toward a new city.

I want to hear the waves slosh on the hull's plates
when we glide in toward the hazy towers and

disige tårne og de gamle broer gjennem røk.

Og jeg vil høre gatenes larm stige,
sporvognene klemte i nye, rare toner.

Jeg vil kjenne lukten av kastanjeknopper
drive mot havnen. Kastanjeknopper og exhaust.

the old bridges at slow speed through smoke.

And I want to hear the street-noise rising,
the trolley cars clanging in new, strange notes.

I want to pick up the smell of chestnut buds
drifting toward the harbor. Chestnut buds and exhaust.

Eftermiddagen

Bilen stanser på hjørnet.
Gaten er hvit og stille.
Gardinenes dovne faner vaier
over en verden av skygge og støv.

Øde er alle spisestuer nu.
Sølvvaser glimter på røde
mahognybuffeter i halvmørke.
På tunge, svaktglødende buffeter i skygge
står kobberfat med frukt.

Nu er det at alle de selsomme mønstre våkner.
Silkeskjermenes påfugl. Broderienes blomsterakre.
Støvsylfidene leker
i skoger av ekeblader. Og fra det kinesiske tempel
strømmer det lav musikk.

Øde er alle spisestuer nu.
Det er timen da du hviler middag, borger.
Bare den store buffeten din lever
og silkeskjermen og blomstervasen.
Mens gulvteppestøvet
danser i strålen fra gatens
nytente lykter.

Båter uler på havnen.
Ute er fortauene våte.

Afternoon

The car stops at the corner.
The street is white and still.
The curtains' lazy banners flutter
over a world of shadow and dust.

All the dining rooms are empty now.
Silver vases glimmer on red
mahogany buffets in half-darkness.
On heavy, faintly shining buffets in the shadows
stand copper plates of fruit.

Now is when all the singular patterns awaken.
The silk screens' peacock. The embroidery's field of flowers.
The dust-sylphs play
in forests of oak leaves. And from the Chinese temple
soft music flows.

All the dining rooms are empty now.
It's the hour when you rest after dinner, burgher.
Only this big buffet of yours is alive
and the silk screen and the flower vase.
While the dust of the carpet
dances in the beam from the streetlights,
just lit.

Boats blow horns in the harbor.
Outside the sidewalks are wet.

Speilglass

På vår seilas med trikken
ut til løvetann og syriner
blev vi sittende fast i speilglass
i en lang osende kanal.

Vi la et blått kjølvann bak oss
gjennem rutenes blinkende brenning
da vi blev hyllet inn i skygge
og så var vi på byens havbund.

Over takenes bølgetopper
så vi maisolen lyse,
men i de hemmelighetsfulle sunkne paradiser
så vi unge piker av voks.

I de strålende, fortryllede akvarier
lå gaudaostenes gule møllestener,
røkelaks
og sprø, duftende roquefort med grønne perler.
Og bak de stirrende speilglass-øine
(fuktige av gatens gjennemtrekk)
korseletter, min herre,
og bysteholdere av silkerips.

La løvetannen lyse.
La trikken seile med sitt kjølvann.
— Jeg er strandet på et koralrev
og lar havets champagne bevifte mine gjellespalter.

Plate Glass

On our sailing trip by trolley
out to dandelions and lilacs
we got stuck in plate glass
in a long reeking canal.
We left a blue wake behind us
through the sparkling surf of the panes
when we got wrapped up in shadow
and found ourselves on the city's sea-bed.

Above the wave-crests of the roofs
we saw the May sun shining,
but in the mysterious sunken paradise
we saw young girls of wax.

In the sparkling, bewitched aquariums
lay yellow millstones of Gouda cheese,
smoked salmon,
and crumbly, fragrant Roquefort beaded with dew.
And behind the staring plate-glass eyes
(damp with drafts from the street)
corsets, dear sir,
and brassieres of ribbed silk.

Let the dandelions shine.
Let the trolley sail with its wake.
— I am stranded on a coral reef
and let the sea's champagne flutter the slits of my gills.

Byens metafysikk

Under rennestensristene,
under de skimlete murkjellere,
under lindealléenes fuktige røtter
og parkplenene:

Telefonkablenes nervefibre.
Gassledningenes hule blodårer.
Kloakker.

Fra østens skyhøie menneskealper,
fra vestens villafasader bak spirea
— de samme usynlige lenker av jern og kobber
binder oss sammen.

Ingen kan høre telefonkablenes knitrende liv.
Ingen kan høre gassledningenes syke hoste i avgrunnen.
Ingen kan høre kloakkene tordne med slam og stank
        hundrede mil i mørke.
Byens jernkledde innvolder
arbeider.

Men oppe i dagen danser jo du med flammende
fotsåler over asfalten, og du har silke mot navlens
hvite øie og ny kåpe i solskinnet.

Og oppe i lyset etsteds står jo jeg og ser hvordan
cigarettens blå sjel flagrer som en kysk engel
gjennem kastanjeløvet mot det evige liv.

Metaphysics of the City

Under the gutter gratings,
under the moldy stone cellars,
under the damp roots of avenues with linden trees
and the parks' lawns:

The telephone cables' nerve fibers.
The gas pipes' hollow veins.
Sewers.

From skyscraping human Alps in the east,
from spirea-hedged façades in the west
— the same invisible links of iron and copper
bind us together.

No one can hear the telephone cables' crackling life.
No one can hear the gas pipes' sick coughing in the abyss.
No one can hear the sewers thunder with slime and stench
        for a hundred miles in darkness.
The city's ironclad entrails
are at work.

But up in the day you, of course, are dancing over the asphalt
with the soles of your feet on fire, and you have silk against
        your navel's
white eye and a new coat in the sunshine.

And up in the light somewhere I, of course, stand and watch
        how
the cigarette's blue soul flutters like a chaste angel
through the chestnut leaves toward eternal life.

Industridistrikt

Det er i jordens oldtid

— at ditt vindu lukkes op mot morgenen
i murbergene
og knirker på sine hasper
og slipper inn lukten av kalk og ny brand
mot dine varme laken,

— at ditt øre fanger den langsomme lyd
av en dampmaskin like i nærheten,
lufthamrenes gjø over takene,
den hule hoste fra gater du ikke kan se gjennem røken,

— at ditt øie møter de store
marker av uld,
jernvanger, tomter med koks
under sparsom sol. Fabrikk-
skorstener med kroner av gul røk,

— at ditt hjerte brister i drøm:
Dinosaurene, hornøglene,
løfter de tynne halser over for-
stenede sumper
og gresser
i skyenes tak av løv,

— at din tanke med ett fylles av lys og våkner:
«Idag skal jeg ut og kjøpe nye sko.»

Industrial District

It is in the earth's prehistory

— that your window is opened to morning
amid mountains of walls
and creaks on its hinges
and lets the smell of lime and new fire drift in
toward your warm sheets,

— that your ear catches the slow sound
of a steam engine nearby,
the jackhammers' barking over the roofs,
the hollow cough from streets you can't see through the
        smoke,

— that your eye meets the huge
fields of dust,
iron meadows, lots with coke
under thin sun. Factory
chimneys with yellow crowns of smoke,

— that your heart bursts into dream:
The dinosaurs, the horned lizards,
raise their thin necks over
petrified swamps
and graze
in the dome of leafy clouds,

— that your mind is filled at once with light and awakens:
"Today I'm going out and buying new shoes."

Jernbaneland

I

Lysfaner henger fra kuppelen ned over boggivogntakene,
Solslyngplantene vifter sakte over kontinentaltoget.
Åtte røksorte boggier dufter cigar og mahogny.

Trallene ramler på stenen. Dampen skjuler oss alle.
Føttene klaprer, mennesker vrimler og snakker.
Veldige lokomotiver opløfter sin vrede stemme.

Strøm gjennem korridorene, tyst over gummiløpere.
Hundrede ansikter her, bak vegger av teak-tre
bleke som voks, lesende, skapt i guds billede.

Speilglassrutene klirrer, svakt knirker boggifjærene.
Snart skal hjulene spille sitt heftige accellerando.
Nu ligger de lydløst og ruger på skinnenes nakke.

*

Godsvogner. Tusen rekker
side om side i søvnen.
Tunge floder som furer
sletten av stål og jern.

Under presenninger
slåmaskiner og tømmer.
Brekkvognenes mørke gate
hvor kornet og fisken bor.

Railroad Country

I

Banners of light from the cupola hang down over the roofs of
  the coaches.
A foliage of heat mirages flutters slowly above the
  Continental.
From eight smoke-black coaches waft the scents of cigar and
  mahogany.

The baggage carts rumble on the pavement. The steam
  envelops everyone.
Feet clatter, people mill around talking.
Powerful locomotives raise up their angry voices.

A streaming through the corridors, muted on the rubber
  runners.
Hundreds of faces here behind walls of teakwood,
pale as wax, reading, made in god's image.

The plate-glass windows rattle, the truck-springs creak
  faintly.
Soon the wheels will play their mighty accelerando.
Now they sit silently brooding on the railhead.

*

Freight cars. A thousand rows
side by side, asleep.
Heavy rivers that furrow
a prairie of steel and iron.

Under tarpaulins
mowing machines and timber.
The boxcars' dark street
where the grain and the fish are.

Tømmer fra duftende skoger
fløtet på langsomme elver,
hugget på moer i måneskinn,
fraktet på sne.

Floder av tre, floder av jern som sover
venter på solopgangens
hvite, smeltende lys.

Da skal skredene løsne,
skinnene gjespe og sprake.
Tusen koblinger strekkes mot milenes sluk.

2

Skinnene, blinkende, brune
grener sig ut over landet
over de tjærete sviller,
gjennem de kløverrøde bakker.

Inn i de klamme tunneller
høit over klirrende broer,
gjennem den øde, ropende mo
hvor timian vifter i gruset,

og gyldenrød tiriltunge
duver ved skinnekanten.
Der snuser den røde vimsende maur
og klatrer i skinnenes rust.

Sanden ligger og lyser
med oljeflekker og mønje.
Mellem de tunge, osende sviller
vokser kamilleblomsten.

Timber from fragrant forests
floated on leisurely rivers,
hewn on moors in moonlight,
hauled over snow.

Rivers of wood, rivers of sleeping iron
wait for the sunrise's
white, melting light.

Then the train-slides will loosen,
the rails will yawn and sparkle.
A thousand couplers will stretch toward the distance's maw.

2

Railroad tracks, brown-tinted, gleaming
branch their way out through the country,
over the tar-blackened crossties,
over the clover-red hillsides.

Into the long clammy tunnels,
high over rattling bridges,
crossing the empty, beckoning moor
where thyme-plants flutter in the gravel,

and golden-red babies' slippers
sway at the roadbed's border.
Poking around, the busy red ant
climbs in the rust of the tracks.

The sand is lying there shining
with red lead and oil-spots.
Between the heavy, reeking crossties
grows the camomile blossom.

*

Det står en snehvit bue
etsteds i skogens arne
og venter med sin høie port
på hjulets kolde klang.

En ensom bro er bygget der,
en tanke spent på hvit granitt
som bærer dig i luftens blå
trygt i sitt store fang.

Et håndtrykk mellem bredder grå
er knyttet hett og varig her.
Et lite vers av stål og sten
i veiens store sang.

*

Inn i tunnellenes hule
følger vi skinnenes reise.
Vannet siler fra taket.
Hit kommer solen aldri.

Vannet siler fra taket
her, under Hjerpetjerns-hovet,
dråpen skraller med ekko.
Hit kommer solen aldri.

Røkens tunge vil slikke
hulens fuktige stener.
Dypt under skogenes røtter
skal sotede tak pile.

Skinnene ligger og venter
boltet og spent over pukksten.
Vannet plasker på svillen.
Hit kommer solen aldri.

*

A snow-white arch is standing
in the center of the forest,
awaiting with its lofty gate
the drive-wheels' chilly clang.

A lonely bridge constructed there,
a thought stretched out on granite, quartz,
supports you in the bluish air,
safe on its giant loin.

The handshake of the two gray cliffs
is sealed here ardently, for good.
A little verse of steel and stone
in the railway's mighty song.

*

Into the holes of the tunnels
we follow the rails on their journey.
Water drips from the ceiling.
Here sunlight never enters.

Water drips from the ceiling
here, under Hjerpetjern Mountain,
droplets clatter with echoes.
Here sunlight never enters.

Tongues of smoke will lap at
the dampened stones of the tunnels
when sooty roofs go scooting
under the roots of forests.

The rails are lying there waiting
bolted and tensed over gravel.
Water splashes on crossties.
Here sunlight never enters.

3

Slik er skinnegangen spent over jorden som en bro.
Slik er hjulenes søvn i den nattlige havn.
Men når dagen bryter frem og når det lysner over mo
skal de grådige åpne sin favn.

Da skal de møtes i en dans, da skal de sprenge sin lyd
i et jagende ridt gjennem skoger og fjell.
Da skal et tusentunget rop som en jublende koral
bryte frem over hjulets propell.

Og hver time på dag og hvert eneste minutt
skal vår jord veltes rundt av den spillende plog.
Og du møter dem ved natt når de skjærer med sitt lys
som en flaggermusving gjennem skog.

Jeg har sovet i et hus som lå like ved en vei
hvor de støvede hurtigtog jager forbi.
Jeg har lyttet til en sang som har dryppet i mitt sinn
en besettende, vill melodi.

Jeg har stanset mine skritt, jeg har stoppet for å se
når den smekre maskin med den glinsende buk
kom og trommet med sin hov over miler av metall
på sitt ridt mot det blinkende sluk.

Jeg har lyttet til dens rop og den kaller mig ved navn
og den kommer til mitt hus som min daglige gjest
og den sier til mitt sinn, du skal selge hvad du har,
være fri som den jagende blest.

For det kommer nok en dag og det kommer nok en tid
da den jord hvor du trår er en brennende jord.

3

That's how the rail line is stretched like a bridge across the
  earth.
Such is the sleep of the wheels in their haven at night.
But as soon as daybreak comes and it lightens on the heath
the greedy cars will open for freight.

Then they will meet in a dance, then they will blast out their
    sound
in a galloping ride across forests and hills.
Then a thousand-tongued cry like a joyous chorale
will break out above the whirr of the wheels.

And each hour by day and each minute by the clock
our earth will be plowed by that musical blade.
And you'll meet it at night when it slices with its beam
like the wing of a bat through the glade.

I have slept in a house that stood just beside a line
where the dusty expresses come racing the grade.
I have listened to a song that has dripped into my mind
an obsessive and wild serenade.

I have stopped in my tracks, I have halted to look
when the slender machine with the glistening ribs
came drumming on its hoofs over endless miles of steel
on its ride toward the flashing abyss.

I have listened to its cry and it calls to me by name
and it comes to my house every day like a friend
and it whispers to my mind, you shall sell what you own,
and be free as the scudding wind.

For there will surely come a day and there will surely come a
    time
when the earth underfoot will be burning coals.

Og du rømmer fra dig selv og da kommer du til mig
på min flukt over syngende spor.

Og du finner ikke ro og du leter overalt
gjennem tider og land i en rivende strøm.
Og du hører mine hjul som en tromme i ditt blod
på din jakt mot den ytterste drøm.

Jeg har sovet i et hus som lå like ved en vei
hvor de gyngende hurtigtog hamrer forbi.
Jeg har lyttet til en sang som har hugget i mitt sinn
en forheksende, vill melodi.

Og jeg hører den ved dag og jeg hører den ved natt
som en bankende knoke av stål på min port.
Og jeg drømte det inatt, og jeg trodde det var sant
at jeg stengte min dør og gikk bort.

And you'll flee from yourself and then you'll come to me
in my flight over singing rails.

And you won't find any peace, you'll be searching everywhere
across ages and lands: a torrential stream.
And you'll listen to my wheels like a drumming in your
      blood
while you hunt for the ultimate dream.

I have slept in a house that stood just beside a line
where the rocking expresses come pounding the grade.
I have listened to a song that has chiseled in my mind
a bewitching and wild serenade.

And I hear it by day and I hear it at night
like a knuckle of steel rapping urgent and rough.
And I dreamt it tonight, and I thought it was real:
that I shut my door and walked off.

fra VRIMMEL

✻ ✻ ✻ ✻ ✻

1935

from SWARM

✻   ✻   ✻   ✻   ✻

1935

Nordlyset

Dagen som stiger med gråt i halsen
bak raggete horisonter er ikke
en virkelig dag, men
alle de døde
forstøtte dager som ikke fant frem til et hjerte.
Nødens dager, sultens og frostens, som
lurer sig hit om natten og prøver
å skinne litt sol og strømme litt lys
fra hungrende, visne bryst.

Fryktsom løfter den
ansiktet nu bak hundrede skoger
og stirrer med brennende øine
ut over riker den ikke fikk lov til å elske.

Nu beveger den sine fingre
og rusker i de svarte sprinkler av natt
og forsøker atter og atter å tende sin osende sol,
men den visner,
svinner og blåses ut av kulden.
Langt ut i vest — ytterst i øst
forsøker den å slippe igjennem, men nattens
murer er bygget av granitt
og dens søiler av stål.

Stirr gjennem rutene,
kom barhodet ut på veiene, og stå
i klynger ved veikryssene:
Langsomt synker den kjempendes armer.
Stum river hun sine klær i stykker,

The Northern Lights

The day that rises with tears in its throat
behind shaggy horizons is not
a real day, but
all the dead
disowned days that didn't make it into anyone's heart.
Days of need, of hunger and chill, which
sneak back here at night and try
to shine a little sun and pour a little light
from starving, withered breasts.

Timidly it raises
its face now behind a hundred forests
and stares with burning eyes
out over kingdoms it wasn't allowed to love.

Now it moves its fingers
and shakes night's black fence-posts
and tries again and again to kindle a smoldering sun
that fades,
dwindles and is blown out by the cold.
Far out in the west — far off to the east
it tries to slip through, but the night's
walls are built of granite
and its pillars of steel.

Stare through the panes,
come out on the roads bareheaded, and stand
in clusters at the crossroads:
slowly the struggler's arms sink down.
In silence she rips her clothes to pieces,

brenner dem så på
kuldens strålende bål.
Røken
blusser op over skogene.
Røken
slår ned over grantoppene og de lave huser på moene.
Røken
fryser til is på himlen, så morgendagen
får grimer av gråt.

then burns them on
the cold's brilliant bonfire.
The smoke
blazes up over the forests.
The smoke
blows down over the tops of spruce and the low houses on
    the moors.
The smoke
freezes to ice in the sky, so tomorrow
is streaked gray with weeping.

Gummi

En hvit morgen i juni klokken fire
da landeveiene ennu var grå og våte
gjennem skogenes uavladelige tunneller,
hadde det gått en bil over støvet
der hvor mauren kom syslende ut med sin barnål nu,
og blev vandrende rundt i det store G i «Goodyear»
som stod presset i landeveissandet
over et hundre og tyve kilometer.
Furunåler er tunge.
Gang på gang gled den med sin vippende last
tilbake
og arbeidet sig op igjen
og skled tilbake igjen.
På reisen frem over det store, skybelyste Sahara.

Rubber

One pale morning in June at four o'clock
when the country roads were still gray and wet
in their endless tunnels of forest,
a car had passed over the clay
just where the ant came out busily with its pine needle now
and kept wandering around in the big G of "Goodyear"
that was imprinted in the sand of country roads
for a hundred and twenty kilometers.
Pine needles are heavy.
Time after time it slid back down with its tottering load
and worked its way up again
and slipped back again.
Outward bound across the great, cloud-illumined Sahara.

Europa

Et ansikt kommer frem av Asia med munnen
åpen og håret kastet tilbake.

Og lar sig kjærtegne av vinden, mens det ler
mot bølgene og snuser inn smaken av salt
som strømmer inn fra de blå sletter.

Dag og natt kan vi høre dets latter fra
kystene: Truende og eftertenksom, spottende
og underfundig, omtrent som den henvendte sig
til noen — vinden, skyene eller til de små
stener som ligger og slipes runde av brenningen.

Europe

A face emerges from Asia with its mouth
open and hair thrown back.

And lets the wind caress it, while it laughs
toward the waves and sniffs the flavor of salt
that streams in from the blue plains.

Day and night we can hear its laughter from
the coasts: Threatening and pensive, derisive
and clever, almost as if it were addressed
to someone — the wind, the clouds or the small
stones being polished round by the breakers.

Arv og miljø

Uskyldig
med store pupiller
og forskrekkede øienbryn
og munnen nysgjerrig spiss
som et barn
går hun til dans
under glatte projektører, kjelne projektører.
Tango og
Cucaracha
til kastanjetter, slik:
Armene løftet. To skritt til siden.
Knekke klosset i knærne.

Nu stirrer
med uskyldige pupiller
og forskrekkede øienbryn
gassmasken ut over verden
med sin snabel nysgjerrig spiss
som et barn.

Så går vi til dans
under kolde projektører, hvite projektører.
Tango og
Cucaracha
til mitraljøser, slik:
Armene løftet. To skritt til siden.
Knekke klosset i knærne.

Heredity and Environment

Innocently
with large pupils
and frightened eyebrows
and her mouth a curious pout
like a child
she begins to dance
under slick spotlights, soft spotlights.
Tango and
Cucaracha
to castanets, like this:
Arms raised. Two steps to the side.
Awkward bend in the knees.

Now
with innocent pupils
and frightened eyebrows
the gas mask stares out over the world
with its snout a curious point
like a child.

Then we begin to dance
under cold spotlights, white spotlights.
Tango and
Cucaracha
to machine guns, like this:
Arms raised. Two steps to the side.
Awkward bend in the knees.

Dirrende telefonstolper

Lyden av stjernenes tunge kvernstener
som skurer langsomt omkring de veldige nav, og
vender de rimfrosne ansikter mot hverandre
og bøier dem bort igjen bak millioner mil,
— alt som beveger sig ute i verdensrummet
på gigantiske kulelagre, utsender lave lyder,
pipende sang som dør av de store avstander.
Dette er det vi hører i bruset fra telefontrådene,
de er antenner som innfanger rummets signaler
og roper dem ut på øde moer om natten
når stolpene står og murrer og kaller urolig
som når et menneske drømmer mørke drømmer
og noe biter i hjertet, kvalfulle tanker
han ikke skjønner, som baner sig vei gjennem strupen,
men stanses av ganen og blir bare brutte rop,
da er det lyden av alle stjernene,
slik tuter det alltid ute i verdensrummet.

Vibrating Telephone Poles

The sound of the stars' heavy millstones
that scrape slowly around the huge hubs, and
turn their hoarfrosted faces toward each other
and bend them away again behind a million miles,
— everything that moves in outer space
on gigantic ball bearings, transmits faint sounds,
a whining song that dies out in the great distances.
This is what we hear in the hiss from the telephone wires,
they are antennae that capture the signals from space
and cry them out over desolate moors at night
when the poles are murmuring and calling anxiously
as when a person dreams dark dreams
and something bites his heart, agonizing thoughts he
doesn't understand, that force their way through his throat,
but are stopped by the roof of his mouth and become only
    broken cries,
that is the sound of the stars,
that's how it always howls in outer space.

fra FJERNTOG

✳ ✳ ✳ ✳ ✳

1951

from Express Train

*   *   *   *   *

1951

Koks

Det raste i koksbøttene
og vi fyrte ovnene med larm dengang,
med lyn og torden morgen, middag og kveld,
og på gatene ramlet hjul med svære aksler,
dundret umåtelig høyt hestevognene.
Det luktet kokegass og fetevarer i Kristiania.
Og koks.

Det var i en damp-tid. Under dens hvite pinsehegger mot
    himlen
og mellem røksøylenes mørke stammer var jeg barn. I deres
    skoger
fant jeg de første kalde blomster: Koks
i Teatergaten.

Coke

A rushing in the coke-scuttles
and we fired the stoves with a racket back then,
with lightning and thunder morning, noon and night,
and wheels with massive axles rumbled in the streets,
the horse-drawn wagons roared terribly loud.
It smelled of cooking-gas and pork in Kristiania.
And coke.

It was an Age of Steam. Under the white cherry blossoms it
      sent toward the sky
and between the dark trunks of its columns of smoke, I had
      my childhood. In their forests
I found the first cold flowers: Coke
in Theater Street.

Kobolt

Farvene er ordenes små søstre. De kan ikke bli soldater.
Hemmelig har jeg elsket dem lenge.
De skal holde sig ved husene og henge opp de klare gardiner
om vår hverdags kammers, kjøkken og alkove.

Den unge Karmosin står mig meget nær, og den brune
Sienna
men ennu mere den tenksomme Kobolt med de fjerne øyne
og det ubetråtte sind.
Vi går i dugg.
Nattehimlen og de sydlige hav
er hennes eiendeler
og et tåresmykke om panden:
Cassiopeias perler.
Vi går i dugg i sene netter.

Men de andre.
Møt dem en junimorgen klokken fire,
når de kommer stormende dig i møte
til morgenbadet i de grønne vikers skum.
Så kan du sole dig med dem på svabergene.
— Hvem vil du eie?

Cobalt

Colors are words' little sisters. They can't become soldiers.
I've loved them secretly for a long time.
They have to stay home and hang up the sheer curtains
in our ordinary bedroom, kitchen and alcove.

I'm very close to young Crimson, and brown Sienna
but even closer to thoughtful Cobalt with her distant eyes and
        untrampled spirit.
We walk in dew.
The night sky and the southern oceans
are her possessions
and a tear-shaped pendant on her forehead:
the pearls of Cassiopeia.
We walk in dew on late nights.

But the others.
Meet them on a June morning at four o'clock
when they come rushing toward you,
on your way to a morning swim in the green cove's spray.
Then you can sunbathe with them on the smooth rocks.
   —Which one will you make yours?

Solsikke

Hvilken såmann gikk over Jorden,
hvilke hender sådde
hjertenes frøkorn av ild?

Som regnbuens striper gikk de av hans never
til tæle, ung muld, het sand,
der skal de sove
grådig, og drikke vårt liv
og sprenge det i stumper
for en solsikkes skyld som du ikke kjenner
eller en tistelkrone eller en krysantemum.

Kom tårers unge regn,
kom sorgs milde hender.
Det er ikke så ondt som du tror.

Sunflower

What sower walked over the Earth,
which hands sowed
our hearts' kernels of fire?

Like rainbow bands they went out from his fists
to frozen soil, young loam, hot sand;
they will sleep there,
voracious, and drink our life
and blast it to pieces
for the sake of a sunflower you don't know about
or a thistle head or a chrysanthemum.

Come, young rain of tears;
come, gentle hands of sorrow.
It's not as terrible as you think.

Fjerntog

Fjerntoget 1256 jager langs bortgjemte, avlåste grender. Hus
efter hus vandrer forbi, gråbleke, hutrende. Skigarder, knauser
og sjø og de lukkede grindene.
Da må jeg tenke i morgendemringen: Hva ville skje om noen
fikk åpne for hjertenes ensomhet? Mennesker bor der, ingen
kan se dem, de går over gulvene, inne bak dørene, nøden, stengte
i øynene, hårde av elskov de ikke kan gi og som ingen får gi
dem.
Hva ville stige høyere her enn fjellene, — Skarvangkampene,
hvilken flamme, hvilken kraft, hvilke stormer av rolig lys?

Fjerntoget 1256, åtte sotsvarte boggier,
svinger mot nye, ustanselig ukjente grender.
Kilder av lys bak rutene, usette brønner av kraft langsmed
      fjellene
reiser vi forbi, haster vi forbi, bare fire minutter forsinket
til Marnardal.

Express Train

Express train 1256 races alongside hidden, remote villages.
House after house wanders by, pale gray, shivering. Rail fences,
rocks and lakes, and the closed gates.
   Then I have to think in the morning twilight: What would
happen if someone could release the loneliness of those hearts?
People live there, no one can see them, they walk across rooms,
in behind the doors, the need, blank-eyed, hardened by love
they cannot give and no one gets a chance to give them.
What would rise higher here than the mountains — the
      Skarvang Hills —
what flame, what force, what storms of steady light?

Express train 1256, eight soot-black cars,
turns toward new, endlessly unknown villages.
Springs of light behind the panes, unseen wells of power along
      the mountains —
these we travel past, hurry past, only four minutes late
for Marnardal.

Mitt tre

Eneren, lyngens mor, er mitt tre.
Den trenger ingen sommer, bare regn og sne.

Fillet krone den løfter, ingen har hørt dens sus.
Den har en lang, seig rot som kan gro av grus.

Den bærer vind over skuldrene, skyene i sitt hår.
Den kan stå i stormen. Knelende. Men den står.

Kanskje den har en drøm i sindet: Det hvite ranunkel-bed
der verden slutter og breene kommer ned.

Av alle trær på jorden nærmest den store sne,
breenes blinde sol. Å, var jeg som det.

My Tree

The cedar, heather's mother, is my tree.
No summer — rain and snow are all it needs.

It lifts a ragged crown; no one has heard its rustle.
It has a long, tough root that can grow in gravel.

It wears wind on its shoulders, in its hair the clouds.
It can hold in storms. Kneeling. But it holds.

Perhaps it has a dream in mind: The white crowfoot-bed
where the world stops and the glaciers descend.

Closest of all trees on earth to the great snow,
the glacier's blind sun. Oh, to be one of them.

Dagen og natten

Endeløs er vår dag.
Den er uten ende.
Den går bare bort til et annet sted,
flytter sig stille bort en liten stund,
slår den blå kåpen omkring sine skuldre,
skyller føttene i havet og går bort,
så kommer den løpende tilbake igjen, med roser på kinn,
og med svale, gode hender
løfter den din hake opp og ser dig inn i ansiktet:
— Er du våken snart?

Endeløs er vår natt.
Den er uten ende.
Den går bare bort til et annet sted
en liten stund,
så er den der igjen
med sine feberøyne
og håret dryppende vått som av sved
og ser på dig, og ser på dig:
— Hvorfor sover du ikke?

Det er ingen ende på fryden, ikke på smerten,
ikke på døden, ikke på livet.
De går bare bort en liten stund, de går rundt jorden
til annet hjerte,
en liten stund,
så kommer de igjen, med sine nølende stemmer:
— Sover du? Er du våken?

Det er ingen ende på stjernene og på vinden.
Det er bare du selv
som ikke er den du tror.

Day and Night

Our day is endless.
It is without end.
It just goes off to another place,
moves off quietly for a little while,
throws the blue coat around its shoulders,
rinses its feet in the ocean and walks off;
then it comes running back again, with roses on its cheeks,
and with good, cool hands
it lifts up your chin and looks you in the face:
— Will you be waking soon?

Our night is endless.
It is without end.
It just goes off to another place
for a little while;
then it's there again
with its feverish eyes
and its hair dripping wet as if with sweat
and looks at you, and looks at you:
— Why aren't you sleeping?

There is no end to delight, none to pain,
none to death, none to life.
They just go off for a little while, they go around the earth
to another heart,
for a little while,
then they come back, with their hesitant voices:
— Are you asleep? Are you awake?

There is no end to the stars and the wind.
There is only you yourself,
who aren't who you think you are.

På Varaldskogen

Det var i den nedre natten, da lyset rant ut mellem skogens
   søyler
og Verdensaltet med ett var kommet helt hit ned til
   Varildbakken
med svart natt helt fra disse grindstolper og frem til Sirius og
Capella,
da sprang det en stjerne frem fra Lebbikø, og enda en fra
Jakobsbakken,
lik en blank nagle slått inn i natten,
og en til
og enda en på nytt berg lenger ut,
at livet skulde bæres frem
ennu en tid.

Og slik, i svart tordnende skog, hvor elg stod nær,
så jeg dem springe frem, en for en, parafinstjernene
i endeløst fjerne berg, og jeg visste da
at slik sprang de frem nu gjennem Gudbrandsdalen
og et lite lys ute på Grip, og i rare mønstre over Nord-Fosen
   og gjennem Bykle-hei,
og jeg så for første gang hvor stort mørket var.

Hvor stort mørket var rundt menneskene, der ensomme
   billykter kom og gikk, som kometene,
sopende sin lyskvast gjennem skoger,
tentes og sluktes ut.

Jeg hilser dere små lys fra Sarjalampi, Vais, Kvindegardslii,
   Vinjebygd,
når lyset er nesten fortapt og bare dette spinkle grindsle
   er igjen
mellem oss og døden,

In the Varald Forest

It was the underside of night, when the light gave out
    between the forest's columns
and suddenly the Universe had come all the way down here
    to Varild Hill
with black night straight from these gateposts out to
    Sirius and Capella;
then a star leapt out from Lebbikø, and yet another from
    Jakobsbakken,
like a shiny nail pounded into the night,
and one more
and still another on a new mountain further out,
that life might be carried on
for another while.

And thus, in black thundering forest, where moose stood
    close by,
I saw them leap forth, one by one, the paraffin stars
on endless distant mountains, and I knew then
that they were springing up now throughout the Valley of
    Gudbrandsdal
and a small light out at Grip, and in strange patterns across
    North Fosen and all through Bykle-hei,
and I saw for the first time how great the darkness was.

How great the darkness was around people, where lonely
    headlights came and went, like the comets,
sweeping their tuft of light through forests,
were lit and were snuffed out.

I salute you, small lights from Sarjalampi, Vais,
    Kvindegardslii, hamlet of Vinje,
when the light is almost lost and only this flimsy
    shield of a gate is left
between us and death;

hilser dere som naglene i vår høye bro gjennem natten
fra kyst til kyst.

Jeg hilser dere lys fra Orion, Antares, Alfa i Centauren,
men hør:
— når jordens bleke stjerner lover dag,
hva lover så Galaksens stjernesky,
Syvstjernens ris og Kosmos tåreslør?
Hva stiger der for glans av neste gry,
hva venter der for dag ved nattens dør?

salute you as the nails in our lofty bridge across the night
from coast to coast.

I salute you, lights from Orion, Antares, Alpha Centauri,
but hear me:
— if the pallid stars of Earth can promise day,
what's pledged by the Galactic cloud of stars,
the Pleiades, the Cosmic mist of tears?
What brilliance of what rising dawn is theirs,
what day is waiting there for night to clear?

fra HEMMELIG LIV

❋ ❋ ❋ ❋ ❋

1954

from SECRET LIFE

❊ ❊ ❊ ❊ ❊

1954

Pavane

Pavanen, denne sære påfugldansen
som infantinnen Isabella danset
med don Juan Fernandez av Castilien
den siste natt før døden gjestet slottet
— likblek og merket alt av kalde fingrer
men kledt i påfuglprakt og med de stive
bizarre skritt som om de alt var døde
— den samme dans som Spanias dronning danset
med hjertet tungt av frykt og halvt forstenet
av tung brokade, pomp og etikette
lik hård emalje om det ville hjertet,
— er det den samme dans som havet danser
med skyene derute, denne stumme
forstemte lek med skyers påfuglhaler
og havets brutte skritt i tung brokade
mot øde himmelhvelv — slik danser havet
til dump musikk en ødslig dans med skyer.

Pavane

Pavane, unique outlandish dance of peacocks
the Infanta Isabella danced for hours
with Captain Juan Fernandez of Castilla
the evening death came calling at the palace
— pale as corpses, marked by chilly fingers
but clothed in peacock splendor, with macabre
and stiffened steps as if they'd died already
— the dance the Queen of Spain was also dancing
with heavy, frightened heart and almost frozen
by dense brocade and pomp and courtly manners
around her untamed heart like hard enamel
— is that the very dance the sea is dancing
together with the clouds out there, this muted
and doleful play, the clouds with tails of peacocks,
the sea in dense brocade with broken movements
toward barren sky — that's how the sea is dancing
a dismal dance with clouds to muffled music.

De store symfoniers tid

De store symfoniers tid
er over nu.

De steg mot himlen i stor prakt
som solskimrende skyer med torden i
over de store århundrer.
Cumulus under lyshimler. Coriolan.

Nu strømmer de ned igjen som regn,
et stengrått, stripet regn over alle bølgelengder og programmer
og dekker jorden som en våt frakk, en sekk av lyd.

Nu faller de ned igjen fra himlen,
de pisker mot skyskraperne som elektrisk hagl
og drypper ned i bondens kammers
og trommer over villabyene og murstenshavet
som evindelig lyd.

Regn som lyd.
Seid umschlungen Millionen,
til å døve skrik

alle dager, alle dager
over jorden som er tørst og tar dem til sig igjen.

The Age of the Great Symphonies

The age of the great symphonies
is over now.

They rose toward the heavens in full splendor
like thunderclouds shimmering in the sun
over the great centuries.
Cumulus under clear skies. Coriolanus.

Now they're pouring back down as rain,
a stone-gray, streaked rain on all wavelengths and programs,
covering the earth like a wet coat, a sack of sound.

Now they're falling back down from the heavens,
they pelt the skyscrapers like electric hail
and seep down into the farmer's bedroom
and drum on the suburbs and the oceans of brick
as eternal sound.

Rain as sound.
Seid umschlungen Millionen,
to deaden screams

every day, every day
on this earth that is thirsty and drinks them in again.

Den ensomme veranda

Langt inne høyt oppe i en stor by hang en ensom veranda,
oppe under skyene hos vinden og som aldri noe menneske
        hadde satt sin fot på
fordi det var så dypt ned og så kaldt derute.

Den syntes den var den ensomste veranda i hele verden
og den hørte klokkespillet hver søndag fra den hellige
        Bartholomeus' kirke,
og den tenkte hvorfor kan ikke den gode Gud hjelpe mig,
han er jo også høyt oppe
og han kunde bruke mig som en liten hylle til å legge sine
        små ting på.
Vestenvinden kjente den best, så bad den vinden spørre.

Da kom et veldig stålstillas og klatrende menn en dag
og de hugget den ned med acetylenflamme på mindre enn 8
        minutter
og hengte opp en sprakende lysreklame i rødt og blått
for Skotsk Whisky.

The Lonely Balcony

Far in and high up in a big city hung a lonely balcony,
up under the clouds with the wind, that no person had ever
    set foot on
because it was so cold out there and such a long way down.

It thought it was the loneliest balcony in the whole world
and it heard the carillon playing every Sunday from Saint
    Bartholomew's Church,
and it thought why can't the good Lord help me,
he too after all is high up
and he could use me as a little shelf to put his knicknacks on.
It knew the western wind best, so asked that wind to inquire.

Then huge steel scaffolds and clambering men appeared one
    day
and they cut it down with acetylene torches in less than 8
    minutes
and hung up a crackling red and blue neon advertisement
for Scotch Whiskey.

Arkeologen

Han skar torven ut med skarp spade
og gravde stenene frem med spiseskjeer
til hjørnene av en boplass kom frem
og restene av et sverd
under falmet aske.

Og det var en grønn og god dag der i skogen,
og da han spiste sine påsmurte rundstykker
tenkte han langsomt mens han tygget at det var
sitt eget hjerte han gravde ut idag
med barneskjeer.

Murrestene han støtte på under der
og stenhjørnet under askelaget
hadde han støtt panden mot før
og fått snudd veiene sine,
hver gang han trodde det skulde gå ham godt i verden.

For det har bodd noen før, tenkte han
dypt nede i mørket mitt.
Det er merkene efter dem
og hellene de la huset på
som er skjebnen min.

Det har bodd noen før i mig
  Ne's sólu sótt ok ne saxi
  steinn skorinn
som i alle mørker og menn.

Han fant også et smykke der med en liten fugl på
og et kjeveben av en hest.

The Archaeologist

He cut out the peat with a sharp spade
and dug up the stones with tablespoons
till the corners of a settlement emerged
and the remains of a sword
under faded ash.

And it was a good green day in the forest,
and when he ate his homemade sandwiches
he thought slowly as he chewed that it was
his own heart he was digging out today
with teaspoons.

The crumbled walls he came upon down there
and the stone corner under the layer of ash —
he had bumped his head against them before,
and gotten turned back
each time he thought that things would go well for him in
    the world.

For people have lived before, he thought,
deep down in my darkness.
The marks they left behind
and the flat rocks they set their house on
are my fate.

Someone has lived in me before
  Ne's sólu sótt ok ne saxi
  steinn skorinn
as in all darknesses and men.

He also found there a piece of jewelry with a little bird on it
and a jawbone from a horse.

Senere gravde han frem en paraply
fra en tid de ikke hadde paraplyer,
og en månedsbillett til Blommenholm
men den var visst hans egen.

Later he dug up an umbrella
from an era when they didn't have umbrellas,
and a monthly railpass to Blommenholm
but that was surely his own.

Tømmer

Det er godt det finnes tømmer enda i verden
og velteplasser nok
enda.
For det er en stor fred i tømmeret
og et stort lys i det
som kan skinne langt inn i kveldene
om sommeren.

Det er god trøst i bråterøk
og i god kvae som trenger ut i store perler
dypt inni skogene.
Lukten av tømmer minner om søt valmue og korn.

Det er godt det lyser av tømmer nok på moene enda
ved Ångermanelven og Deep Creek, Columbia,
som en søle efter solstrålene
rundt om i verden,
en sovende styrke på jorden, en hemmelig kraft
som skal vare i slektsledd, nesten som jern.

Det har brødets farve og kvinnekroppens
og den skinnende viljen i sig
som kanskje kommer av stor kjærlighet.

For tømmeret er en del av den store våren i verden.
Det kommer fra kilder som ødeleggeren enda ikke har nådd.

— — —

Det er de store elvene som tar sig av det.
Er det en elskov mellem treets kraft og vannets?
De fører det sakte rundt store nes i en stille rytme som
minner om dans.

— — —

Timber

It's good that there is still timber in the world
and still enough places along its course
for stacking it up.
For there is a great peace in timber
and a great light in it
that can shine far into the evenings
in summertime.

There is good solace in smoke from clearings
and in rich sap that wells out in big pearls
deep in the forests.
The smell of timber recalls sweet poppies and grain.

It's good that the barrens from the Ångerman River to
Deep Creek, Columbia still shine
with timber like a slick of sunbeams
all around the world,
a sleeping force on earth, a secret power
that will last for generations, almost like iron.

It has the color of bread and of women's bodies
and has about it the shining will
that perhaps derives from great love.

For timber is part of the great Spring in the world.
It comes from sources the ravager still hasn't reached.

— — —

The large rivers look after it.
Is there a love between the wood's power and the water's?
They lead it slowly round high headlands in a calm rhythm
    that reminds one of dance.

— — —

Det er disse ting stjernehimmelen er satt over:
De dødes ensomhet, ungdommens mot og tømmer
som føres langsomt avsted på store elver.

These are the things the starry sky is set above:
Loneliness of the dead, courage of youth, and timber
 that's carried slowly away on great rivers.

Skytsengelen

Jeg er fuglen som banker på vinduet til dig om morgenen
og følgesvennen din, han du ikke kan vite,
blomstene som lyser for den blinde.

Jeg er brekronen over skogene, den blendende
og malmstemmene fra katedralenes tårn.
Tanken som plutselig faller ned over dig midt på dagen
og fyller dig med en besynderlig lykke.

Jeg er en du har elsket for lenge siden.
Jeg går ved siden av dig om dagen og ser ufravendt på dig
og legger munnen på hjertet ditt,
men du vet det ikke.

Jeg er den tredje armen din og den andre
skyggen din, den hvite,
som du ikke har hjerte til
og som ikke kan glemme dig mere.

Guardian Angel

I am the bird that knocks at your window in the morning
and your companion, whom you cannot know,
the blossoms that light up for the blind.

I am the glacier's crest above the forests, the dazzling one
and the brass voices from the cathedral towers.
The thought that suddenly comes over you at mid-day
and fills you with a singular happiness.

I am one you have loved long ago.
I walk alongside you by day and look intently at you
and put my mouth on your heart
but you don't know it.

I am your third arm and your second
shadow, the white one,
whom you don't have the heart for
and who cannot ever forget you.

De gamle damer

De unge kvinnene med lynsnare føtter, hvor blir det av dem?
De som har knær som små kyss og sovende hår.

Langt ute i tiden når de er blitt stille
gamle damer med smale hender og går langsomt i trappene

med store nøkler i vesken og ser sig omkring
og snakker til små barn ved kirkegårdsportene.

I det fremmede store landet hvor vintrene er lange
og ingen mere skjønner deres sprog.

Bøy dig dypt og hils dem med ærbødighet for
de bærer det med sig enda som en duft,

et hemmelig bitt i kinnet, en nerve inne i
håndflatene etsteds som røper dem.

The Old Ladies

The young women with lightning-quick feet — what happens
    to them?
The ones who have knees like small kisses, and sleeping hair.

Much further along when they've become quiet
old ladies with slender hands and go slow on the stairs

with huge keys in their bags, and look around
and talk to little children by the churchyard gates.

In the vast foreign country where the winters are long
and no one understands their language anymore.

Bow deeply and greet them with respect, for
they carry it with them still, like a fragrance,

a hidden bite inside their cheeks, a nerve deep in
their palms somewhere that gives them away.

Alderdommen

Jeg holder mere av de gamle.
De sitter og ser på oss og ser oss ikke
og har nok med sitt eget,
som fiskere langs store elver,
stille som sten
i sommernatten.
Jeg holder meget av fiskere langs elver
og gammelt folk og de som kommer ut efter lang sykdom.

De har noe i øynene
som verden ikke ser lenger
de gamle, lik rekonvalesenter
som føttene ikke er sterke nok under enda
og med bleke pander som efter feber.

De gamle
som blir sig selv igjen langsomt
og løses opp langsomt,
som en røk, umerkelig går de over
i søvn
og lys.

Old Age

I'm very fond of old people.
They sit looking at us and don't see us
and are content on their own,
like fishermen along big rivers,
still as stone
in the summer night.
I'm quite fond of fishermen along rivers
and old folks and those who come out after long illnesses.

They have something in their eyes
that the world doesn't see anymore,
old people — like convalescents
who aren't steady enough on their feet yet,
foreheads pale, as after fever.

Old people
who become themselves again slowly
and are slowly dissolved,
like a haze, imperceptibly, they melt
into sleep
and light.

Den omvendte sommeren

Det brenner også en annen sommer på jorden
den omvendte, som vokser nedover i mørket
som speilbildet i de stille sjøene.

Den har hengende trær og hvitt gress,
alt vridd som av hemmelige vinder.

Vet jeg hvor virkeligheten er? Er jeg
rot eller er jeg krone. Er det ikke stjerner
også der, av svakt lysende sten?

The Inverted Summer

There's a second summer burning on the earth —
the inverted one, that grows downward in the dark
like the mirror image in the still lakes.

It has hanging trees and white grass,
all twisted as if by secret winds.

Do I know where reality lies? Am I
root or am I crown. Aren't there stars
there too, made of faintly shining stone?

Midtsommernattens lys

Midtsommernatten er ikke en riktig natt,
det er en galskap i den, en is rundt hjertet
fra en angst ute bak skogene et sted,
noen som vil skrike men kan ikke få frem et ord.

Måltrostens vanviddsfløyte
tørster efter salighet men kan ikke få den.
Lyset er fylt av noen som vil gråte i det,
som har lagt blomstene igjen på marken
og skjuler det hvite ansikt i hendene.

Midtsommernattens lys
skingrer bak skogene og over sjøenes is
som de glitrende øynene på den avsindige,
som steg og steg svimlende gjennem sol
og blomstenes røk, men kjenner først i natt
i denne time i sitt kjøds begjær
at han er av dødens ætt.

Midsummernight's Light

Midsummer Night isn't a proper night,
there's a lunacy in it, ice around the heart
from a dread out behind the woods somewhere,
someone who wants to scream but can't get a word out.

The song thrush's crazy warble
thirsts for salvation but cannot get it.
The light's poured out by someone who wants to weep in it,
who's left the flowers behind in the field
and is hiding his white face in his hands.

The light of Midsummer Night
screeches behind the woods and across the lake-ice
like the glittering eyes of the madman,
who climbed and climbed dizzily through sun
and the flowers' perfúme, but first senses tonight,
in this hour in the lust of his flesh
that he is one of death's tribe.

Turnipshøst

Det er tungt dette som vi løfter opp av jorden her
som mursten og marmorpostamenter
efter det store soltemplet til Vitsilopochtli.
Grav mer, her er gudinnens lår
mørke av jord. Bær dem bort.

Turnip Crop

It's heavy, what we lift from the earth here
is heavy as bricks and marble pedestals,
remnants of the great sun-temple of Huitzilopochtli.
Dig more, here are the goddess's thighs
dark with earth. Carry them off.

Sorgfulle tårn

Slavene hadde veldige hender og bygde sorgfulle tårn.
De hadde hjerter av bly og skuldre som fjellvegger og bygde
sorgfulle tårn.
De hadde hender som stenhammere og bygde berger av
taushet.

De står i Burgund og Baalbek og Xeres de la Frontera.
Askegrå murer over skogene, pander av sten og tungsindige
øyne,
mange steder på jorden
hvor svaler går ut i store sløyfer i luften
som lydløse svepeslag.

Mournful Towers

The slaves had powerful hands and built mournful towers.
They had leaden hearts and shoulders like rocky cliffs and
    built mournful towers.
They had hands like sledgehammers and built mountains of
    silence.

They stand in Burgundy and Baalbek and Jerez de la Frontera.
Ash-gray walls above the forests, foreheads of stone and
    melancholy eyes,
in many places on the earth
where swallows dash out in wide loops in the air
like silent strokes of a whip.

Stavkirker

Jeg tror på de mørke kirkene,
de som ennu står som tjærebål i skogene
og bærer duft med sig som de dyprøde rosene
fra tider som kanskje eide mer kjærlighet.
De sotsvarte tårnene tror jeg på, de som lukter av solbrannen
og gammel røkelse brent inn av seklene.
Laudate pueri Dominum, laudate nomen Domini.

Øksene teljet dem til og sølvklokker klang i dem.
Noen skar drømmer inn og ga dem vinger å vandre med
ut gjennem tider og fjell. De velter som brottsjø omkring dem.
Nu er de skip, med utkikkstønnene vendt mot Ostindia,
Santa Maria, Pinta og Niña da dagene mørknet
mot verdens ende, årelangt fra Andalusia.
Laudate pueri Dominum, laudate nomen Domini.

Angst overalt, selv Columbus er redd nu
der hildringer lokker dem frem og vinden har slangetunger.
Stjernene stirrer urørlige ned med avsindige jernøyne,
alle dager er onde, det er ingen redning mer, men vi
seiler, seiler, seiler.
Laudate pueri Dominum, laudate nomen Domini.

Stave Churches

I believe in the dark churches,
the ones that still stand like tarred pyres in the woods
and like deep red roses carry a fragrance
from times that perhaps had more love.
Those jet-black towers I believe in: the ones that smell of the
    sun's heat
and old incense burnt in by the centuries.
    Laudate pueri Dominum, laudate nomen Domini.

Axes shaped them all and silver bells rang in them.
Someone carved dreams in and gave them wings so they'd
    wander
out across ages and mountains — which surge up around
    them like breakers.
Now they are ships, with crow's nests turned toward East
    India,
the Santa Maria, Pinta and Niña when the days grew dark
near the end of the world, years out from Andalusia.
    Laudate pueri Dominum, laudate nomen Domini.

Everywhere dread, now fear takes even Columbus
when mirages lure them on and the wind has the tongues of
    a serpent.
The stars stare down impassively with demented eyes of iron,
every day is evil, there is no more salvation, but we
keep sailing, sailing, sailing.
    Laudate pueri Dominum, laudate nomen Domini.

fra SOMMEREN I GRESSET

✳ ✳ ✳ ✳ ✳

1956

from S U M M E R I N T H E G R A S S

❁   ❁   ❁   ❁   ❁

1956

Månen og apalen

Når apalen blomstrer
kommer ofte månen som en blomst,
blekere enn dem alle
og lyser over treet.

Det er den døde sommeren,
den hvite søsteren til blomstene som kommer igjen
for å se til oss
og lyse fred med sine hender,
at det ikke skal kjennes tungt når ilden kommer.

For Jorden selv er en blomst, sier den,
på stjernenes tre,
blek og med blad
av lysende hav.

The Moon and the Apple Tree

When the wild apple blossoms
often the moon shows up as a flower,
paler than the rest,
and shines above the tree.

It is the dead summer,
the flowers' white sister coming back
to visit us
and proclaim peace with its hands,
so the fire to come won't be too hard for us.
For the Earth itself is a flower, it says,
on the tree of stars,
pale and with petals
of luminous ocean.

Gamle menns graver

Gamle menns graver
er som ungdommens graver
ganske stille og med solhvite sten,
men det er mere av jord i dem
og dypere ensomheter
i gravene til gamle menn.

Større himmel er det også i dem
og mildere sol eftersom alle ting
vender tilbake til sig selv.
Derfor skulde det stå store trær
med susende kroner hvelvet
over gamle menns graver.

Old Men's Graves

Old men's graves
are like the graves of youth,
quite still and with sun-bleached stones,
but there is more Earth in them
and deeper loneliness
in the graves of old men.

There is also bigger sky in them
and milder sun, insofar as all things
turn back into themselves.
Therefore great trees should stand
with rustling crowns vaulted
over old men's graves.

Nattfugl

Kråkene er nattens fugler.
Tungt kommer de ut av demringen
og speider på oss med stenkullsøyne
hele dagen og med hårde skrik,
at vi ikke skal fortape oss i lyset.

Tunge skygger over takene,
mørke vinger på rutene
binder trådene sammen
fra natt til natt.

Nightbird

Crows are the birds of night.
Ponderously, out of the dawn, they come
and guard us with anthracite eyes
all day and with harsh calls,
so we won't lose ourselves in the light.
Heavy shadows over the roofs,
dark wings on the windowpanes
tie the threads
from night to night.

— En annen sol

Det er en annen sol
ute bak solen og et annet lys
tvunnet inn i alle stråler.
Den brenner ikke rød, den brenner hvit.

Det er en annen sol
større enn vår et sted bak lyset.
Den glitrer som smeltende sne
i øynene på den vanvittige.

Det er noen som er brent av en annen sol.
De har øyne som sne og stemmer
bak dører av jern
og har lys av et annet lys.

Det som hugger øynene ned til roten
så de ikke kan flytte blikket mere
eller se forbi
som du.

Smertenes sum i verden.
Sorgens sol, den hvite
kvikksølvflammen høyt
over alt lys.

Sol bak solen. Flamme for alt hvitt i verden:
liljene, sneen, visdommen.
Se konvallen i gresset, liljen i skogen
— hvorfor gjemmer den sig under høye trær,
dypt
i skyggen av løv?

— A Second Sun

There is another sun
out behind the sun and another light
twined into every beam.
It doesn't burn red, it burns white.

There is another sun
larger than ours, somewhere behind the light.
It glitters like melting snow
in the eyes of the crazed.

There are some who are burnt by another sun.
They have eyes like snow and voices
behind iron doors
and draw light from another source.

The kind that chops the eyes down to the root
so they can't shift their gaze anymore
or look beyond
like you.

The sum of all the pain in the world.
Sorrow's sun, the white
quicksilver flame high
above all light.

Sun behind the sun. Flame for everything white in the world:
lilies, snow, wisdom.
Look in the woods at the lily of the valley
— why does it hide under tall trees,
deep
in the shade of leaves?

Grønt lys

Dyr som knitrer i skyggen, alle de skjeve,
forvokste i verden, de med bittesmå ben og altfor mange øyne
kan gjemme sig i gresset, derfor er det til,
lydløst og fullt av måneskinn mellem kontinentene.

Jeg har bodd i gresset hos de små som ligner knekket kvist.
Humlene kom fra sine tårn av soleihov som klokker
inn i mitt hjerte med ord av magisk art.
Vindene tok mitt dikt og bredte det ut som støv.

Jeg har bodd i gresset hos Jorden og jeg har hørt den puste
lik et dyr som har gått langt og er tørst efter vannhullene,
og jeg kjente den legge sig ned om kvelden tungt på siden
        som en bøffel
inne i mørket mellem stjernene hvor det er plass.

Vindenes dans og de store løpeildene i gresset husker jeg ofte:
— Skyggebildene av smil i et ansikt som alltid har tilgivelse.
Men hvorfor den har så stor tålmodighet med oss
dypt inne i jernkjernen, det store magnesiumshjertet,
        det skjønner vi ikke på lenge.

For dette har vi glemt, at Jorden er en stjerne av gress,
en frø-planét, rykende av sporer som skyer, fra hav til hav,
et fokk. Frø biter sig fast under brostenene
og mellem bokstavene i mitt dikt, her er de.

Green Light

Creatures that rustle in the shadows, all the crooked
deformed ones in the world, with tiny feet and far too many
      eyes,
can hide in the grass — that's why it's there,
silent and full of moonlight among the continents.

I have lived in the grass among the small ones who resemble
      broken twigs.
From their towers of cowslip the bumblebees came like bells
into my heart with words of a magic species.
The winds took my poem and spread it out like dust.

I have lived in the grass with the Earth and I have heard it
      breathe
like an animal that has walked a long way and is thirsting
      for the waterholes,
and I felt it lie down heavily on its side in the evening
      like a buffalo,
in the darkness between the stars, where there is room.

The dance of the winds and the great wildfires in the grass
      I remember often:
— The shadow play of smiles on a face that always shows
      forgiveness.
But why it has such great patience with us
deep down in its iron core, its huge magnesium heart, we are
      far from understanding.

For we have forgotten this: that the Earth is a star of grass,
a seed-planet, swirling with spores as with clouds, from sea to
      sea,
a whirl of them. Seeds take hold under the cobblestones
and between the letters in my poem, here they are.

Fossestøperen

En mann i Norge. Han som
synger bak skogene støtt
og tumler med jern.

Høyt i kløfter
henger han med smiene sine.
Det ryker der.

Klang er over alt
av den usynlige mann.
Han som helder malm i sjø
og gråsten i juvene,
men får det ikke til.

Alltid bak skogene
hører vi hamrene hans, ding — dong.
Men det går opp i luften og blir bare sang av det
og blått lys oppi granbaret
som hos troll.

The Foundryman of Waterfalls

A man in Norway. The one who
constantly sings beyond the forests
and grapples with iron.

High up in crevices
he hangs with his forges.
It's steamy there.

Everywhere, the sound
of this invisible man.
Who pours ore into the sea
and granite into canyons
but is never done.

Always beyond the forests
we hear his hammer, bing — bong.
But it melts in the air and becomes only song
and blue light up in the pine branches
as among the trolls.

Sjøspeilinger

Når vannene er åpne i Norge
kommer fjellene langsomt frem og titter.
De legger sig på kne og stuper hodene nedi,
tett i tett med berg og skogbryn. Se på dem
som polfarere efter syv parafinvintre,
svette i pelsene nu og kåte vasser de uti
mellem skyenes våte selskjær og isbjørnunger
i alle vannenes åpne råk.

Vann nok! Det er ikke en fjellknark noe sted
som ikke kan dyppe trynet i en sjø
og finne en hvit fisk der og leke litt
om sommeren.

Hå. En liten vannknupp vil jeg finne, jeg òg.
Det er godt for tankene, sier yoghien,
å stå på hodet nedi der en stund
og trekke skyene i halen.

Mirror Lakes

When the lakes have thawed in Norway
the mountains come out slowly and peek.
They get down on their knees and plunge their heads in,
crowding hilltops and the edges of forests. See them as
polar explorers after seven winters of kerosene,
randy now and sweating in their furs they slosh out
between the clouds' wet seal-rocks and polar bear cubs
in all the open channels of the lakes.

Water enough! There's not a mountain geezer anywhere
that can't dip his mug in a lake
and find a white fish there and play a little
at summer.

Aha. I'll find myself a little bud of water too.
It's good for the mind, says the yogi,
to stand on your head down there awhile
and tow the clouds by their tails.

Hvor går gatene hen?

Hvor går gatene hen
når det ikke er noen sporvogner i dem,
bare støv og brente fyrstikker?
De må være her ved slaktehuset
og ved melkebarene hele tiden,
tørre og grå
står de og biter i stakittene
til langt på kveld.

Det er så mange fattige gater i verden
med bare parallelle sten,
fra gassklokkene til slaktehuset
og en kafé med stoler og disk.

Det er gater som har tapt på forhånd
fordi de har for meget cement i hendene
og for tunge hjerter
fra fødselen av.

Where Do the Streets Go?

Where do the streets go
when there aren't any trolleys in them,
only dust and burnt matches?
They have to stay here by the slaughterhouse
and the dairy bars forever,
dry and gray they
keep chewing on the picket fences
till late in the evening.

There are so many poor streets in the world
with only rows of paving stones,
from the gas lamps to the slaughterhouse
and a café with a counter and stools.

There are streets that have lost in advance
because they have too much cement in their hands
and hearts too heavy
right from birth.

Billedhuggeren

Marmorets hvite tårer
drypper over billedhuggerens hender
når han løfter de kolde somrene frem til oss,
stenenes rosenbilder, all flyktet form
henter han ut igjen fra frost — to kvinneskuldre
en pikes bleke skjød, en pande av sorg
tar form igjen og stenene drypper ned
som tårer over hånden alle dager.

Men nettene lenges nu og han hører redd
i sitt eget bryst en hammer slå,
en meisel banke. Hva finner du her for trekk,
tenker han titt. Hva fanger du nu, min Gud,
og hvilke former
løfter du frem av mig med dine hender
når alle splinter, all min frost er falt?

The Sculptor

The marble's white tears
drip over the sculptor's hands
when he lifts the cold summers out for us;
the stones' rosy images, all vanished form
he teases out again from frost — two womanly shoulders
a girl's pale bosom, a forehead of sorrow
take shape again and the stones drip down
like tears over his hand every day.

But the nights lengthen now and frightened he hears
a hammer strike, a chisel tap
in his own breast. What sort of features will you find here,
he often thinks. What are you capturing now, my God,
and what forms
will you lift out of me with your hands
when all the shards, all my frost has fallen?

I gobelinsalen

Ignazius og Bonaventura, de høye gobeliner
med sitt lys av gammelt sølv og fordervelse,
jeg skulde gjerne bo i dem et århundre
blandt kyrassene der, med maven full av høyfrø,
det kunde kanskje dempe min ærgjerrighet
som har bragt mig helt til Venezia.

For hva skal vi gripe til, vi som leker med støv
når alle de gamle låvene er borte
og alle somrene i dem, de som sovnet med hånd under kinn der
og alle duftene omkring sig som lysstripen over et solefall.

Men i dette høygulvet kan vi leve sølvgrå
i de store bingene her hos Ignazius og Bonaventura,
de er falmet litt mellem hellebardene
men dufter vilt ennå
av Timian og Botticelli. Europas låve
med all den spøkelsesaktige herlighet som stiger opp av
gammel urett.

Her løfter Roland hornet mellem fjellene,
bare som en duft nu og tre tråder med ull,
men jeg har en fløyte her som bare fuglene kan skjønne
og nu kaller jeg dem ned fra skogene som Fransiscus,
se, de setter sig rundt mig i lyttende ringer når jeg spiller
    for dem
om vindenes lek og de grønne skyggene i gresset
til jeg sender dem tilbake igjen til skogene av støv.

La mig da få komme inn i gobelinet
og legge min vindfløyte ned mellem skyggene der,

In the Hall of Gobelin Tapestries

Ignatius and Bonaventure, the great Gobelins
with their sheen of old silver and ruin —
I'd gladly live in them a century
among the cuirasses, with my belly full of hayseed;
perhaps that would subdue my ambition,
which has brought me all the way to Venice.

For what shall we fall back on, we who play with dust,
when all the old barns are gone
and all the summers in them, those who fell asleep there
    with hand under cheek
and all the odors around.them like the shaft of light above a
    sunset.

But in this hayloft we can live, silver-gray,
in the huge bins here at Ignatius and Bonaventure's;
they have faded a bit between the halberds
but still smell of wild
thyme and Botticelli. Europe's barn
with all the ghostly glory that rises up from
ancient injustice.

Here Roland lifts his horn among the mountains,
only a fragrance now and three woollen threads,
but I have a flute here that only the birds can understand
and now I'm calling them down from the forests like
    St. Francis —
look, they settle around me in circles and listen when I play
    for them
about the frolic of wind and the green shadows in grass,
until I send them back again to the forests of dust.

Let me come into the Gobelin, then,
and lay my wind-flute down among the shadows,

så spiller den sakte de bleke trådene av tid
til kløverknekt og rosmarin, en dis om skuldrene.
Jeg som likte så godt å velte rundt i gammel kløver,
la mig få gå på hodet inn
i høstens herlighet en gang til
med ansiktet i fioler.

where it will slowly play the pale threads of time
to rosemary and garlanded knave, a mist about their
    shoulders.
I who liked so much to roll around in old clover,
let me enter autumn's splendor once more,
head first,
my face in the violets.

fra BREV TIL LYSET

❋ ❋ ❋ ❋ ❋

1960

from LETTER TO THE LIGHT

❋ ❋ ❋ ❋ ❋

1960

Brev til lyset

Morgenens papir er veldig foldet ut
på jorden, det er en ny dag
og en traktor som alt er fremme med sin klumpete neve
og skriver et brev til lyset, hver bokstav
brummer den høyt for seg selv, for det har meget å si
at alt kommer med, både tordnen og biene,
maurveien som har strukket ut sin lille
silkefot i gresset, vår fred
og den uro vi har med alt, skal den ha med.

Store fuktige linjer og en langsom hånd
som ryster svært men nu er alt sagt,
siden er full og alt legges åpent frem
som et brev til ingen, plogenes brev
til lyset som den kan lese som vil.

Letter to the Light

Morning's paper is splendidly unfolded
on the Earth, it is a new day
and a tractor is already out there with its lumpy fist,
writing a letter to the light, growling
each letter aloud to itself, for it's important
to get everything in, the thunder and the bees,
the ant trail that's extended its little
silken foot in the grass, our peace
and the unease we feel about everything — it has to get
all these in.

Large moist lines and a slow hand
that shakes a lot but now it's all said,
the page is full and everthing's laid out in the open
like a letter to no-one, the plow's letter
to the light that anyone who wants to can read.

I januar

O alt hva du kan i januar
når alle dagene bare rekker deg til knes
og du går døgnet rundt og støter panden mot stjernene
som på et loft med gamle uniformer.
I januar da verden er full til overmål av levende sne
som møter deg med glade bjeff mot ruten
og legger seg lydig ned foran alle dører ut
som en stor vennlig hund
som kommer med tungen og vil slikke deg skarpt på
   hendene.

I januar
når alt er stengt og alle veier muret med cement
og du kan gå ut og lage huller i den med begge ben
og gjøre nesten alt. Gå ut eller være i ro,
rydde en skuff
og finne sky og meget unge billeder der
som du kan brenne — eller vente litt.

Og ta en bok i hånden, blåse litt støv
og bøye bladene tilbake i sin ro
som lette snefall. Brev
med stive skrifter, håndtrykk
over havet der vi kom fra, hit
til landet uten lyd
hvor alt er ens og alle ansikter er flate
som tallskivene på ur, de trekker øyenbrynet opp
når du har tenkt en utålmodig tanke.

Hva kan du mer i januar,
når alle ord er snakket døde

In January

O all the things you can do in January
when the days come no higher than your knees
and you keep bumping your head against the stars day and
 night
as in an attic full of old uniforms.
In January when the world is overflowing with live snow
that meets you with happy barks against the windowpane
and lies down obediently in front of all the exits
like a big friendly dog
that comes with its tongue out and wants to lick you roughly
 on the hands.

In January
when everything's closed and all the roads have walls of
 cement
and you can go out and make holes in it with both feet
and do almost anything. Go out or stay in,
tidy up a drawer
and find shy and very young pictures there
that you can burn — or wait a bit.

And take up a book, blow off some dust
and thumb the pages back to rest
like a light snowfall. Letters
with stiff writing, hands touching
across the ocean where we came from, to this
land without sound
where everything's the same and all faces are flat
as the faces of clocks, they raise their eyebrows
when you've thought an impatient thought.

What more can you do in January,
when all words are talked to death

og ligger strødd omkring som krøllete aviser
og alle sår er bundet om med gaze
og alle spor er vasket bort
og du kan gå rundt og høre plankene knirke
og ovnene knurre rolig over sine kjøttben.

— Sett deg. Legg ut din store kabal
som aldri går opp og spør
hva du kan gjøre for ditt hjerte mere enn det.
By det en mørkere tobakk? Klyve opp på en stige
og heise en drabelig røk som et flagg opp fra din skorsten
til glede for skyene som kommer drivende nu fra Karelen
med underlige forrevne bryst,
for å ruge de nye dager ut
og den lille gule sol du snart får se
på gjerdestolpene i februar.

Men nu i januar — da skal du vente på ditt hjerte.
La stjernene bare klirre ved din seng. Du ser
en pande komme frem, et ansikt i nordlyset.
Bak blygrå gardiner setter hun frem sin lave lampe
ved puten din så hun kan se på deg
om dine trekk er blitt forandret.

all lie strewn about like curled-up newspapers
and all wounds are bound up with gauze
and all tracks are blotted out
and you can walk around and hear the boards creaking
and the heaters softly growling over their meat-bones.

— Sit down. Lay out your great game of solitaire
that never works out and ask
what more you can do for your heart than that.
Offer it a darker tobacco? Climb a ladder and raise
a bold flag of smoke from your chimney
to delight the clouds that come driving in now from Karelia
with strangely ragged breasts
to hatch the new days
and the little yellow sun you'll soon see
on the fenceposts in February.

But now in January — now you must wait for your heart.
Let the stars go on rattling by your bed. You see
a forehead emerging, a face in the northern lights.
Behind lead-gray curtains she sets her dim lamp out
near your pillow so she can see
if your features have been changed.

Nattvindu

Et vindu mot natten og isnende høyt der ute
ser jeg en stjerne stå som en ørn i skyer
ute ved verdens grense der alle rop forstummer.
Kanskje den venter på mitt hjerte nu eller en annens,
men vindushaspene er på og nattens møll vil inn
med tusen hender og gripe fatt i mitt lys
som den druknendes rop, men det forgår,
vingene knuses og alle er døde snart.
Det store farveslam efter solen er vasket ut
og natten høy og stum, jeg hører
ditt rolige åndedrett der du går omkring i søvnens hus,
de store rum hvor jeg ikke kan komme inn.
Du flytter på ting som er kommet ut av sin fred,
rydder i skap og på bord og jeg kan merke
ditt ansikt derinne, din pande bak gardinet
med forandrede trekk og øyne jeg ikke kjenner.

Men hånden er ikke med, den ligger ute
på teppet som din lille vakthund, halvt sovende
halvt våken og det ene øret løftet opp
mot mine tanker.

Nu er den tredje time da alt levende er kommet i hus
og stjernene kommer ned for å holde råd på jorden,
med stenharde øyne, ubevegelige som fugler
står de i ring om våre hus som ved et tingsted
og dømmer til døden eller til livet det som er hendt
og det som skal skje i morgen legges klart for alle.

Men din pust er rolig som en isnende kilde
hvor tankene sildrer nesten lydløst forbi mot elven

Night Window

A window on the night and freezing high out there
I see a star hanging among clouds like an eagle,
out at the border of the world where all cries die down.
Perhaps it's waiting for my heart now, or another's,
but the window hasps are latched and the night-moths want
    to come in
with a thousand hands and grab hold of my light
like the drowning man's cry; but it passes,
their wings are broken and soon they've all died.
The slush of color spread by the sun is washed out
and the night high and still, I hear
your steady breathing as you walk around in sleep's house,
the large rooms I cannot enter.
You shift things that have been disturbed,
tidy up closets and table and I can make out
your face in there, your forehead behind the curtain,
with changed features and eyes I don't know.

But your hand hasn't joined in, it's lying outside
on the blanket, your little watchdog, half asleep
half awake with one ear pricked up
toward my thoughts.

Now is the third hour, when all living things are at home
and the stars come down to hold council on Earth;
with eyes hard as stone, unmoving as birds
they stand around our house in circles as at an ancient moot
and sentence — to death or to life — what has happened,
and what must happen tomorrow is made plain to everyone.

But your breathing is quiet as a spring freezing over,
where the thoughts trickle by almost soundlessly toward the
    river

over røtter og de lave stener i din drøm
hvor skyggeaktige fisk står snute mot snute sovende
med vidåpne øyne bak de store grå-hellere der,
eller i de klare hvelv på bunden. Det er en gate mot havet
der jeg er bregnen og den lave hyldegren
som fanger inn sitt disige billede her
hvor ingen krusning ennå gjør linjene forandret
og kanskje en stjernes stål forviller seg også dit.
Som en ørn med glitrende nebb venter den på mine øyne.

across roots and the low rocks in your dream
where shadowlike fish hang sleeping snout to snout
with wide-open eyes behind the large blocks of slate,
or in the clear vaults at the bottom. It's a street to the sea
and I am the ferns and the low elder-branch
that take in their foggy picture
where no rippling changes the lines yet,
and perhaps the blade of a star will go astray here too.
Like an eagle with glistening beak it waits for my eyes.

Nu bærer elven sine lamper ut

Nu bærer elven sine lamper ut.
Stenbildet dypt i bekker
som vannets hender lenge ville skjule,
trer rolig frem som skår av keramikk

der pander av kisel bøyes mot kalkstensskuldre
og viser oss klart at ingenting skal vare
mer enn en hastig tid, et åndedrett mot kinnet,
et streif av flyktende leber nu før lampene bæres ut

og stenbildet kommer frem i de tørre bekker
som brune skår og skall av knuste vaser.
De var av ler, de var for spinkelt bygget
for denne sols umåtelige ild.

Now the River Is Carrying Off Its Lights

Now the river is carrying off its lights.
The stone-picture deep in streams
that water's hands tried to hide for so long
calmly appears as pottery shards

where silica foreheads lean toward limestone shoulders
and show us clearly that nothing will endure
more than a brief time, a breath on the cheek,
a touch of fleeing lips now before the lights are carried off

and the stone-picture appears in the dry streams
as brown shards and the shells of broken vases.
They were of clay, they were too fragile
for this sun's intense fire.

Minnet om hester

Linjene i de gamles hender
bøyer seg langsomt og peker snart mot jorden.
Dit tar de med sitt hemmelige sprog,
skyenes ord og vindenes bokstaver,
alle de tegn som hjertet samler opp i armodens år.

Sorg blekes ut og vender seg til stjernene
men minnet om hester, kvinneføtter, barn
strømmer fra deres ansikter over i gressets rike.

I store trær kan vi ofte se
billeder av dyreflankers ro,
og vinden tegner i gresset, hvis du er glad,
løpende barn og hester.

The Memory of Horses

The lines in old people's hands
bend over slowly and soon point toward the earth.
They take their secret language there with them,
words from the clouds and letters from the winds,
all the signs the heart gathers up in impoverished years.

Sorrow bleaches out and turns to the stars
but the memory of horses, women's feet, children
streams from their faces into the grass's kingdom.

In large trees we can often picture
the calm of animal flanks,
and the wind draws in the grass, if you are happy,
running children and horses.

Små lys på havet

Din hånd som hviler her, er en hvelvet båt
halvt trukket opp på stranden
og full av åndedrag som en konkylie
venter den på deg at du skal komme tilbake.

Og jeg kan se at enda er noen ute
på havet som snart er helt mørkt nu
— fiskere som har tent lys i båter
som bølgeryggene langsomt løfter opp
og langsomt ned igjen som om de lette
med lamper, myggefine foran et mektig lerret
om de kan finne ut av den ubegripelige signatur
eller lyse et ansikt frem,
en farve som gir håp.

Small Lights at Sea

Your hand at rest here is an upturned boat
pulled halfway onto the beach,
and full of breathing as a conch's shell
it waits for you to come back.

And I can see that someone is still out
on the ocean that will be completely dark soon
— fishermen who've turned on lights in boats
that the crests of waves bear slowly up
and slowly down again as if they were searching
with lamps, small as gnats before a great canvas,
to make out the undecipherable signature
or bring to light a face,
a color that offers hope.

Gamle ur

Gamle ur har ofte vennlige ansikter
og kan minne om bønder fra skogbygder og fjell
med en rolig likesælhet i sitt vesen
som om de hørte til en annen slekt enn vår

som kanskje har stridd ut sin tid hernede
og sett sin uro visne ned som gresset
i sine store skar og stille myrstrøk
forrige gang Jorden var til.

Nu er de gjester her og nikker til vår kummer
med lavmælt visdom ved vår seng: Det går,
ja, ja, det går, det går.

Old Clocks

Old clocks often have friendly faces
and can remind us of farmers from forest country and
      mountains,
a calm disinterest in their bearing
as if they belonged to a different race from ours

that perhaps has struggled through its time down here
and seen its uneasiness wilt like the grass
in great chasms and still marshlands
the last time Earth existed.

Now they are visitors here and nod to our sadness
with low-voiced wisdom by our bed: It's all right,
yes, yes, all right, all right.

Tausheten i trær

Om natten når de små orkestre reiser hjem
og alle trommene er trette av å tromme
står høye trær langs gatene som porter
av lydløshet, som høye kandelabre
foran et gotisk univers vi ikke fatter.
De gylne saksofonene blir pakket ned
som baby-dolls på rosa silkeputer
— bildører slår igjen med korte smell
og drosjer piler bort i øst og syd
— den store tuba surres fast på taket
some en dukke-elefant med store ører
og klovnen reiser hjem
og sangeren med det store kalciumsmil
og Clarissa, nakendanserinnen, reiser hjem
for å kle av sitt hjerte foran søvnens ansikt,
hver sigarettglo lukker trett sitt øye
og alt blir slettet ut av nattens tavle
med lydløs hånd
så tausheten i trær skal komme frem.

For snart skal alle lyd i verden hjem og sove
og alle farvene bli trette av å farve
og reise bort fra oss til ukjent sted
og alt skal viskes ut med myke kluter
som nu inatt med det støvfine regn som sølv
over alle parker ruvende som porter
inn til et rike vi engang dro bort fra
og tausheten skal bryte frem
i alle trær.

The Silence in Trees

At night when the small orchestras travel home
and all the drums are tired of drumming,
tall trees stand along the streets like gates
of soundlessness, like high candelabras
before a Gothic universe we do not grasp.
The golden saxophones are packed away
like dolls on pink silk cushions
— car doors slam shut with brief bangs
and taxis dart away to east and south
— the big tuba is lashed down on the roof
like a toy elephant with huge ears
and the clown goes home
and the singer with the big calcium smile,
and Clarissa, the nude dancer, goes home
to unclothe her heart before the face of sleep,
each cigarette glow tiredly shuts its eye
and everything is erased from night's slate
by a soundless hand
so the silence of trees will come out.

For soon all the sounds in the world will go home and sleep
and all the colors will get tired of coloring
and travel away from us to unknown places
and everything will be rubbed out by soft cloths
as now, tonight, by powdered-silver rain
over all the parks looming like gates
to a kingdom we once parted from
and the silence will break out
in all the trees.

Tårnene i Bologna

Tårnene i Bologna, de to
som bare står og står i en luft av sølv
og luter seg nesten umerkelig mot hverandre
fordi de er trette av tiden og stjernenes tog ustanselig.

De strekker langsomt sine skygger ut mot verden
for å prøve forsiktig hvor langt all tid er kommet,
kjenner på torvenes blå druer og solpikenes bryst om de er
        hårde
og føler seg sakte frem langs alle murers revner
til tårnenes flaggermus, og kirkeklokkenes malm.

Blått regn kommer og svinger milde flagg over deres ansikter
— den store lombardiske fane og syv bannere
fra Piazensa og Modena, men de husker dem ikke lenger.
Alt er kommet så langt ut og de er nesten blinde
i et land hvor solen knurrer som en tiger mot alle
og fyller våre lunger helt tilbunds med truslen om
        sønderrivelse,
der morgenen kommer og strør sitt fattige salt på fortauene
og piker med brune kinn kommer ned i portene
nesten opphovnet i munnen av for meget natt.

Asinelli og Garisenda, de to
hellende tårn som går rundt over byen med sine skygger
som et slags langsomt ur med sine visere

The Towers in Bologna

The towers in Bologna, those two
that just stand and stand in silver air
and lean almost unnoticeably toward each other
because they are tired of time and the stars' constant
     procession.

Slowly they stretch their shadows out toward the world,
carefully testing how far time has come,
touch the markets' blue grapes and the sunshine girls' breasts
     to see if they're firm
and feel their way slowly forward along the cracks in all the
     walls
to the bats in the towers, and the brass of the church bells.

Blue rain comes and swings soft flags across their faces
— the large banner of Lombardy and seven pennants
from Piacenza and Modena — but they don't remember them
     anymore.
Everything's come such a long way and they are almost blind
in a land where the sun growls at everyone like a tiger
and fills our lungs to the bottom with the threat of
     dismemberment,
where morning comes and sprinkles its poor salt on the
     pavements
and girls with brown cheeks come down into the doorways
with mouths almost swollen by too much night.

Asinelli and Garisenda, those two
leaning towers that sweep across the city with their shadows
like a kind of slow clock with its hands pointing

for timene av elskov og forferdelse, hva sier tiden,
hvor langt er det kommet med alle.

Hver dag må de se
damen i porselensbutikken som tørrer støv med silkekluter
hvor de små bjeller har spinkle lyd som sølv
og de ser bussjåførene som går bort og røker cigar i
    skyggen av sine tårn,
mødre som gir småbarn bryst i dem,
og gamle ektefolk som kan hate hverandre i mørket fra disse
    tårn,
de springende og jagende som kan være nervøse i dem,
slakteren som hugger opp sine koteletter,
prestene som leser sitt officium
i skyggene fra Asinelli og Garisenda
evighetens tårn, litt trette av å være
mann og kvinne, dag og natt, og vise
altets dobbelte natur, det tvedelte liv
som lengter efter forening
som de store trær lengter efter aftnen i skogen
og den store endeløse stjerne.

to the hours for love and anxiety: what does time say,
how far gone are things for everyone.

Every day they have to see
the lady in the china shop who dusts with scraps of silk
where the little bells have fragile sounds like silver
and they see the bus drivers who go off and smoke cigars in
     the shadows of their towers,
mothers who nurse their babies in them,
and old husbands and wives who can hate each other in the
     dark of these towers,
the hurriers and scurriers who can be nervous in them,
the butcher who chops up his cutlets,
the priests who read their Office
in the shadows of Asinelli and Garisenda,
eternity's towers, a bit tired of being
man and woman, day and night, of showing
the duality of the universe, the divided life
that longs for union
as the great trees long for evening in the forest
and that large, enduring star.

Katakombene i San Callisto

En by i døden med gatene styrtet inn og trafikklysene stumme.

En by sett i et knust speil som vi må gni mørket av med
hendene.

Under stjernene og under jorden, en by som en latter bak en
lukket dør.

Et Venezia av natt, broer som speiler seg i støv.

Verdens stolthet, en by med panden kløvet og ansiktet grodd
ned med slam.

Tynne rottrevler som fingre og føtter, hender og skulderblad
av skjeletter.

Røtter og grener av røtter, døde som bøyer fingrene om
mørket som rundt en sten.

Et tre opp av vår knuste virkelighet med roten plantet i
fornedrelse.

Et tre som strekker grenene ut over jorden og rekker nesten
til stjernene, Arcturus, Capella.

Et tre fra jordens hjerte. Forundring. Trofasthet.

The Catacombs in San Callisto

A city in death with the streets caved in and the traffic lights still.

A city seen in a broken mirror we have to rub the darkness from with our hands.

Beneath the stars and beneath the earth, a city like a laugh behind a closed door.

A Venice of night, bridges reflected in dust.

The world's pride, a city with its forehead split and its face overgrown with slime.

Thin shreds of roots like fingers and feet, hands and shoulder blades of skeletons.

Roots and branches of roots, dead that bend their fingers around the dark as around a stone.

A tree up from our broken reality, with its root planted in humiliation.

A tree that stretches its branches out over the earth and reaches almost to the stars, Arcturus, Capella.

A tree from the earth's heart. Wondrous. Keeping faith.

fra STILLHETEN EFTERPÅ———

❋ ❋ ❋ ❋ ❋

1965

from THE SILENCE AFTERWARDS———

❊ ❊ ❊ ❊ ❊

1965

Langsomt———

Bilder av umåtelige land,
sandflukter, bronceaktige himler
skal stå til tidenes ende, vinden
løfter det lille sandkornet opp på en sten,
regnværet skyller det bort.

Således er jordens ansikt mellem stjernebildene
dekket av glemsel—langsom
som stenene er Guds gjøren med oss,
en dag skal komme som en rose—en dag som en ild.
Alt har sin tid.
Om tusen år
er sneglen kommet frem til treet.

Jeg ser et gammelt regnvær gå bøyd over aftenens land
og lete med tynne hender efter de glemte ting,
det ingen enser mer—stillheten mellem strå,
halvsagte ord, bruddstykker av fortapthet, tanker
nesten ingen har tenkt, de tause
veier av gress og søvn som fører frem
fra tid til tid.

Hvor finner vi nu
det som kan binde sammen det spredte.
Stien i stjernene, kompassnålens veier
eller linjene i alle pikers hender
som ligner vinden gjennem rosene.
For det er sent

snart bærer elven mine bilder ut,
åssider, speilinger av hus, et elsket ansikt
bærer den ut til havet. Alt skal ryddes

Slowly ——

Images of measureless lands,
sand dunes, bronzelike skies
will last till the eons end; the wind
lifts the little sand-grain onto a stone,
rain washes it away.

This is how the earth's face among the constellations
is covered by forgetfulness — slowly:
God's dealings with us are as slow as the stones.
One day will come like a rose — one day like a fire;
everything has its time.
In a thousand years
the snail will have reached the tree.

I see ancient rain walking bent across evening's land
and searching with thin hands for the forgotten things,
what no one notices anymore — the stillness between blades of
    grass,
half-uttered words, fragments of loss, thoughts
almost no one has thought, the silent
roads of grass and sleep that lead forward
from age to age.

Where do we find now
a way to connect what is scattered.
The path in the stars, the compass needle's roads
or the lines in girls' hands
that are like the wind through the roses.
For it is late

soon the river will carry off my images;
hillsides, reflections of houses, a beloved face —
it will carry them out to sea. Everything will be cleared off

uten et ord og kloden bøyer
rolig sin skulder mot natt og dag.
Et sted suser vinden alt morgenen inn i skogene,
et sted går omrisset av en bergvegg umerkelig inn i natten.

without a word and the planet will calmly
turn its shoulder toward night and day.
Somewhere the wind is already rushing morning into the
forests,
somewhere the outline of a rocky cliff passes gradually into
night.

Stillheten efterpå

Prøv å bli ferdige nu
med provokasjonene og salgsstatistikkene,
søndagsfrokostene og forbrenningsovnene,
militærparadene, arkitektkonkurransene
og de tredobbelte rekkene med trafikklys.
Kom igjennem det og bli ferdige
med festforberedelser og markedsføringsanalyser
for det er sent,
det er altfor sent,
bli ferdige og kom hjem
til stillheten efterpå
som møter deg som et varmt blodsprøyt mot panden
og som tordenen underveis
og som slag av mektige klokker
som får trommehindene til å dirre
for ordene er ikke mere til,
det er ikke flere ord,
fra nu av skal alt tale
med stemmene til sten og trær.

Stillheten som bor i gresset
på undersiden av hvert strå
og i det blå mellemrommet mellem stenene.
Stillheten
som følger efter skuddene og efter fuglesangen.
Stillheten
som legger teppet over den døde
og som venter i trappene til alle er gått.
Stillheten
som legger seg som en fugleunge mellem dine hender,
din eneste venn.

The Silence Afterwards

Try to be done now
with the challenges and the sales statistics,
the Sunday brunches and the combustion furnaces,
the military parades, the architectural competitions
and the six lanes with traffic lights.
Come through that and be done
with party preparations and market-research analyses,
for it is late,
it is much too late,
be done and come home
to the silence afterwards
that meets you like a warm spurt of blood against your
        forehead
and like thunder rolling
and like strokes of mighty bells
that set your eardrums quivering,
for words don't exist anymore,
there are no more words,
from now on everything will speak
with the voices of stone and tree.

The silence that lives in the grass
on the underside of each blade
and in the blue space between the stones.
The silence
that follows the shots and the birdsong.
The silence that lays a blanket over the dead man
and that waits in the stairwell till everyone's left.
The silence
that lies like a baby bird between your hands,
your only friend.

Nattemørket

Nattemørket overlever i krokene
mellem gulvbjelkene og i stengte skap
til det skal bre seg ut over verden.
Vi pisker natten med våre lys,
neon og ildkaskader over gatene
og driver det ut i skogene og ned i gresset.
Men det kommer igjen
i våre hjerter, inne mellem fryktens bjelker,
nede i uvisshetens gress
venter det på timen da det skal slå ut sin mørke vinge
fra Sirius og til bunden av det siste hav.

The Dark of Night

The dark of night survives in the niches
between floor beams and in closed closets
until it's time to spread out over the world.
We pelt the night with our lights,
neon and fiery cascades across the streets,
and drive it out into the woods and down into the grass.
But it comes back
in our hearts; inside, between the timbers of fear,
down in the grass of uncertainty
it waits for the hour when it will spread its dark wing
from Sirius to the bottom of the last ocean.

Tanker ved avlytting av
et radioteleskop

Da radioen sendte lydopptak av stjernestøyen
fra universet CO-35m i Centauren, verdens ytterste
kom visergutten inn med varene fra kjøpmannen
— Det er no galt med apparatet Deres, hører jeg.

Noe galt med apparatet. Jo vi kan høre
verden brenne der ute, men det er flammer av kulde
fra dommedager lenger ute enn døden
som falmet til støv endog før lyset fødtes.

Og eldre enn Sagenetrikken, ufattbare tiders
vandringer er endt i denne lenestol på en torsdag
like før pinse med lokaltoget syv minutter forsinket,
køer i butikkene og en skurring i apparatet

der stjernen vedblir å tale med støtvise ord og hutrende
bruddstykkevis fra de dødes rike til de levendes
men kablene er sprengt og vi forstår ikke
tid eller sted for noe er hendt med oss

og vi famler i blinde. Dette
er kyster vi aldri har sett, kanskje tidsaldre
bak mørkets teppe, dimensjoner
like ved vårt ansikt som kan forandre alt.

Kanskje et ekko av oss selv, konkyliesuset av våre kriger
eller bølgeslagene fra et hav under menneskets hjerte.
— Hva skal vi tro.

Seil spennes ut i natten — våre drømmer,
ukjente skip går forbi
på hav ingen kan se.

Thoughts upon Listening In
on a Radio Telescope

When the radio broadcast recordings of the noise of stars
from Galaxy CO-35m in Centaurus, the most distant known,
the delivery boy came in with the packages from the grocer
— There's somethin' wrong with your set, sounds like.

Something wrong with the set. Yes, we can hear
the world burning out there, but it is flames of cold
from doomsdays further out than death
that faded to dust even before the light was born.

And older than the Sagene trolley, wanderings through
inconceivable ages have ended in this easy chair on a Thursday
just before Pentecost with the local train seven minutes late,
lines in the shops and a burring on the set

where the star goes on with its shivering words,
speaking in snatches from the realm of the dead to the living
but the cables are broken and we do not understand
time or place, for something has happened to us

and we grope blindly. These
are coasts we have never seen, perhaps eons
behind the blanket of darkness, or in dimensions
just beside our face that can change everything.

Perhaps an echo of ourselves, the conch-shell rush of our wars
or the wash of waves from an ocean under the human heart.
— What shall we think.

Sails are unfurled in the night — our dreams;
unknown ships go by
on oceans no one can see.

Tankeløs —

Inne i alle dager er det et lite hjerte
og en åpen hånd.
Kanskje hver dag er et liv for seg.
Morgenen har sin lov og aftenen har sin
og om natten er det en krone av ild over vårt hus
ingen kan nå.

Sommerbekkens lille hvite pande
er full av tanker den ikke kan holde fast på
og hører til i en annen verden, krystallren
men flyktigere, alltid musikk.

Grankonglen faller ned som et gongongslag
og noen netter er fulle av et bronceaktig lys.
Ørreten vandrer i sin elv som et spor
av fruktbarhet dypt i hjertet, den har
en munn som gaper og svelger uten å drikke.

Til denne verden hører også kvinnenes små lykker:
en katt i fanget, lave ord til barn
og alt som vokser, trådene i en vev,
tre fingerspor på vinduene om aftenen,
det er for smått til å nevne men det er
kanskje det lave gresset i vårt liv,
den grønne bølgen som skyller om strandens sten
og bekken med den hvite panden,
tankeløs, full av muskk.

Unthinking —

Within every day there is a small heart
and an open hand.
Perhaps each day is a life in itself.
The morning has its law and so does the evening
and at night there is a crown of fire above our house
that no one can reach.

The summer brook's little white brow
is full of thoughts it can't hold onto
and belongs in another world, crystal pure
but more fleeting, always music.

The spruce cone falls like the stroke of a gong
and some nights are full of a bronzelike light.
The trout wanders in its river like a trail
of fertility deep in the heart, it has
a mouth that gapes and swallows without drinking.

To this world too belong women's small delights:
a cat in the lap, low words to children
and everything that grows, the threads on a loom,
three finger-tracks on the windows in the evening —
they are too small to name but they are
perhaps the low grass in our life,
the green wave that washes around stones on the beach
and the brook with the white brow,
unthinking, full of music.

Avignon, Vaucluse

Under skyenes cumulus-tre en by på sletten
med mørke brystvern og tårnenes knudrede kuber.

Som et underlig hus i mørkningen. Guds bier
stillet ut under skyenes tre, mellem valmuene og vinen.

Summende av liv er den i aften, myldrende i alle vinkler
som en rasende bisverm når den ikke kan finne honningen.

Den har bannere i gull og sort, ridderrustninger med jernklør
og solens giftbrodd satt inn midt mellem øynene.

Men selv i de dypeste gater er det gullskjær over husene
som minner om voksplatene i tømte bikuber, sier du.

Om natten kom regnet. Da klokkene brummet midnatt
ble alt sløret til av et underlig røkflor, som silketøy.

Og dette, sier du vennlig, er biavlerens slør og hansker.
Nu tar han ut honningen og setter inn sukkervannet.

Avignon, Vaucluse

Under the clouds' cumulus-tree, a city on the plains
with dark breastwork and the towers' knobby hives.

Like a curious house in the dusk. God's bees
set out under the tree of clouds, between the poppies and
 the vine.

It's buzzing with life this evening, teeming in every corner
like a furious swarm of bees when they can't find the honey.

It has banners of gold and black, knight's armor with iron
 hands
and the sun's poisonous sting stuck right between its eyes.

But even in the deepest streets there is a golden sheen to the
 houses
that recalls the plates of wax in emptied beehives, you say.

At night the rain came. When the bells thrummed midnight
everything was veiled in a strange misty crepe, like a garment
 of silk.

And this, you say amiably, is the beekeeper's veil and gloves.
Now he's taking out the honey and putting in the sugar-water.

fra HEADLINES

❄ ❄ ❄ ❄ ❄

1969

from HEADLINES

❋ ❋ ❋ ❋ ❋

1969

Ventetid

Noen står ute i solen og venter andre
venter ved bensinstasjoner kaféer
er gode å vente i du kan sitte
og tenke på hva som kan hende
om det ikke inntreffer
det du er redd for håper på
er likegyldig med iallfall
ventetid
i sykesengen på oboslisten eller
i billettkøen alderdoms-
hjemmet men mest
venter vi på det
som aldri hender eller
hender hver dag like-
gyldig gutt eller pike eller
på døden rikstelefonen
og postmannen men mest
på det som gjør glad
det lille
du holder gjemt i hånden
det lillelille
du holder skjult
forsiktig
i den ene hånden.

Waiting Time

Some stand out in the sun and wait others
wait at gas stations cafés
are good to wait in you can sit
and think about what can happen
if what you're afraid of hope for
are indifferent to doesn't
happen at any rate
waiting time
in the sickbed on the Oslo Housing list or
in the ticket-line the old-age
home but mostly
we wait for what
never happens or
happens every day un-
important boy or girl or
for death the long-distance call
and the mailman but mostly
for what gladdens
the little
you keep hidden in your hand
the little little
you hold hidden
carefully
in one hand.

Bonde-norge

Fjellene på frontruten, så sandelig
der dukker de opp igjen
bonde-norges grå støvler, veltet i haug.
— Selv er de under torven men støvlene
ligger her efter dem
gråe av støv, tungt regn og sorg.
Vindusviskerne vasker dem ikke bort.

Selv ute i havet ligger det hauger av steinstøvler
— tusener av dem — som fjell,
kaldvasket, skjeve og grå.
Hauger av døde
dager, hauger av år.
Vindusviskerne
vasker dem ikke bort.

Peasant Norway

With the mountains in the windshield, I swear
they pop up again:
peasant Norway's gray boots, piled in a heap.
— They themselves are under the sod but the boots
still lie here
gray with dust, heavy rain and sorrow.
The windshield wipers don't wash them away.

Even out in the sea there are heaps of stone boots
— thousands of them — like mountains,
washed by cold water, crooked and gray.
Heaps of dead
days, heaps of years.
The windshield wipers
won't wash them away.

Noen

Noen
stiger ut av vårt liv, noen
kommer inn i vårt liv
ubedt og setter seg ned,
noen
går likegyldige forbi, noen
skjenker deg en rose,
kjøper en ny bil,
noen
står deg meget nær, noen
har du alt glemt,
noen, noen
er deg selv,
noen
har du aldri sett, noen
spiser asparges, noen
er barn,
noen går opp på taket,
sitter ved et bord,
ligger i hengekøye, går med rød
paraply,
noen ser på deg,
noen har aldri lagt merke til deg, noen
vil holde deg i hånden, noen
døde i natt,
noen er andre, noen er deg, noen
er ikke,
noen er.

Some

Some
climb out of our lives, some
come into our lives
unasked and sit down,
some
pass by indifferently, some
present you with a rose,
buy a new car,
some
are very close to you, some
you've already forgotten,
some, someone
is yourself,
some
you have never seen, some
are eating asparagus, some
are children,
someone is going up on the roof,
sitting at a table,
lying in a hammock, walking with a red
umbrella,
some are looking at you,
some have never noticed you, some
want to hold your hand, some
died tonight,
some are others, some are you, some
are not,
some are.

Vintertegn

Frosten knytter hendene og vil sprenge veibanene i stykker.
Aspenes løv er drept med formalinkapsler.
Is-breene sleper seg skritt for skritt over dal-toppene
tunge i baken og forpustet — en meter på tusen år.
Skyene er grimet av tretthet, varmer sine fingre
på en mørkerød sol. Fuglene
har tømt sine trær og reist bort i avmakt. Tungen
vender seg innover i din gane.
Tanken låser sin dør.

Signs of Winter

Frost clenches its fists and tries to shatter the roads.
The aspen leaves die with formaldehyde on their breath.
The glaciers drag themselves step by step across the heads of
     valleys,
bottom-heavy and winded — a meter every thousand years.
The clouds are streaked with fatigue, warm their fingers
on a dark-red sun. The birds
have left their trees empty and gone away defeated. Your
     tongue
curls back on your palate.
Thought locks its door.

Veis ende

Veiene er nu kommet til enden,
de kommer ikke lenger, de snur her,
borte på jordet der.
Det er ikke mulig å komme lenger hvis
De ikke vil til månen eller planetene. Stans nu
i tide og bli til hvepsebol eller ku-tråkk,
vulkanrør eller steinrammel i skogene
— det er det samme. Noe annet.

De kommer ikke lenger har jeg sagt
uten forvandling, motoren til hesteromper plutselig
girstangen til en grankvist
som De holder slapt i hånden
— — hva faen var dette?

Road's End

The roads have come to the end now,
they don't go any further, they turn back here,
over at that field.
It's not possible to go further if
you don't want to go to the moon or the planets. Stop while
there's time and become wasp's nest or cow path,
volcano's vent or rockslide in the forest
— it doesn't matter. Something else.

You can't go any further, I've said,
without transformation: the motor into a horse's rump
    suddenly
the stick shift into a pine branch
that you hold loosely in your hand
— — what the hell is this?

Til Iris

Farvene bor hos deg
bare hos deg
grønt gult indigo og fiolett
bare hos deg — i øyet ditt
inne bak smilet der, utenfor er allting
natt avskyelig av elektroner
farveløst — helt blåst.
Bare hos deg — inne bak øyet der
er farvene til.
Tenk på det.

Hele regnbuen er hos deg
(bare regnværet hos meg)
farven på kjolen din, negle-
lakken, rosen, dåpsattesten
bare i øyet der
og ikke utenfor.
Tenk på det.

Det er øynene dine som kler verden på
— grønt, gult, indigo og fiolett
— bukser jakke sko og kam i håret.
Tenk på det.

To Iris

The colors live in you
only in you
green gold indigo and violet
only in you — in your eye
in there behind your smile; outside everything is
night abominable made of electrons
colorless — totally bare.
Only in you — in there behind your eye
do the colors exist.
Imagine that.

The whole rainbow is in you
(only rainfall in me)
the color of your dress, nail-
polish, rose, birth certificate
only in your eye
and not outside it.
Imagine that.

It is your eyes that clothe the world
— green, gold, indigo and violet
— pants jacket shoes and the combs in your hair.
Imagine that.

fra PASS FOR DØRENE —

DØRENE LUKKES

❋ ❋ ❋ ❋ ❋

1972

from W ATCH THE DOORS —

THE DOORS ARE CLOSING

✻ ✻ ✻ ✻ ✻

1972

Grønn mann

Gå
sier den grønne mannen i trafikklyset
til alle bukseben bag'er barnevogner
brilleglass og brystholdere, få med deg
bena for nå haster det
med verden med vesten med østen med
varehuskjeder vinimport vekselfrister vel-
standsutvikling vannforurensning og voff-
voff. Få med deg bena, kom over for nå ...

Stopp
sier den røde mannen
som er den samme som den grønne
mannen men i rødt, stille nå
og se hvor langsomt det går
med verden og vreden og vold-
somheten og vantrivselen
når de andre skal prøve seg. Stille
nå, helt stille, med solreiser og
sommerhusplaner. Hold kjeft nå men
bare i førti sek ...

Gå
sier den grønne
gå bare gå
med deres verden voldtekt
valium og vacuumpakninger.
Gå
— dere har
i nøyaktig astronomisk tid
bare førti sekunder.

Green Man

Go
says the green man in the traffic light
to all the pant-legs shopping-bags baby-buggies
glasses and brassieres, get
a move on because now it's urgent
for the world for the west for the east for
department-store chains wine-imports exchange-deadlines de-
velopment of affluence water pollution and woof-
woof. Get a move on, come on over because now . . .

Stop
says the red man
who is the same as the green
man but in red, quiet now
and see how slowly change comes
to the world and the fury and the
vehemence and the dissatisfaction
when the others are having a go. Quiet
now, completely quiet about holidays in the sun and
plans for the summer house. Shut up now but
only for forty sec . . .

Go
says the green
go just go
with your world rape
valium and vacuum-packing.
Go
— you have
in precise astronomical time
only forty seconds.

Angelus

Mirakler som hender omigjen
er ikke lenger mirakler
blir snart likegyldigheter som ansikter i en buss
eller den frosne elven av stjernelys
som strømmer langsomt over huset ditt om natten
også når du er død og opptatt av andre ting.
Hva vet du om dette. Det gamle
du ser deroppe statisk og fosforskimrende
er kanskje verdens sperma, Guds sæd, som flommer
og jorden den du står på er cellen
den ene den benådede
med fosterhinnen og med fødselsskriket.
«— Se han har sett sin tjenerinnes ringhet,
Fra nå skal alle slekter prise mig salig.»

Men vi skal dø snart og det gjelder å få med seg alt
bil kone og gressklipper og ikke tulle seg bort
med tanker som gjør deg rar. Alle har sitt.
Men av og til kan vi jo lure på
hva som egentlig foregår her.
For hva skal vi tro på da. Gamle historier
eller nye historier. Tusenårsriker eller Hva
sier stjernene.

Best ikke å hefte seg. For noe kan hende snart.
Og det gjelder å få med seg alt
som tyven sier
når huset tilfeldigvis står tomt
og det bare er en eldgammel sol
og en blindfødt måne som holder vakt.

Angelus

Miracles that happen over again
are no longer miracles,
soon become inconsequential like faces in a bus
or the frozen river of starlight
that flows slowly over your house at night
and will go on when you are dead and concerned with
    other things.
What can you know about all this. The old light
you see up there, unchanging and phosphorescent,
is perhaps the world's sperm, God's seed flowing
and the earth you are standing on is the cell
the one, the favored one
with the birth sac, the cry of birth.
"— Behold he hath regarded the low estate of his
    handmaiden;
from henceforth all generations shall call me blessed."

But we will die soon and the point is to get hold of
    everything
car wife and lawnmower and not get lost
in thoughts that make you odd. We all have our problems.
But once in a while we can certainly wonder
what is really going on here.
For, what shall we believe in anyway. Old stories
or new stories. The Millennium or
Your Horoscope.

Best not to take notice. For soon something may happen.
And the point is to get hold of everything
as the thief says
when by chance there is no one in the house
and only an ancient sun
and a moon blind from birth
are standing watch.

Briefing

Gud sa: De små.
La dem komme til meg.
Pst! Alle små. Over her. Still i kø
små hender silkesokker tanker
lys og luft små ord og gjerninger
små hus små land små dyr og blomster
revebjelle og linnea. De store
lar vi seile. Alle små
velkommen vær. Ikke så redde da.
Kom så.
Kom så. Og ta kanarifuglen med
for nå må vi tenke litt
på det som skjer. Vi må
bli sterkere på jorden støere
på bena ellers tar de oss
og putter oss i sekken
alle sammen — efter tur
hver silkesokk hver skygge lys og luft
alt som gjør jorden grønn
og himlen blå
små hus små land små brev
og små bokstaver bier
og maur og metemark
blås ikke bort men bli
hvor dere står.
Pass godt
på hodene.
Slipp ikke taket. Husk på
at jorden snurrer
rundt og rundt
og rundt og rundt
og at alt som er
kommer igjen
— også jeg. Sa Gud.

Briefing

God said: The small ones.
Let them come unto me.
Psst! All small ones. Over here. Line up
small hands silk socks thoughts
light and air small words and deeds
small houses small countries small animals and flowers
foxglove and honeysuckle. We'll let
the big ones make their own way. All small ones
feel welcome. Not so afraid, then.
Come on.
Come on. And take the canary with you,
because now we have to think a bit
about what's happening. We must
be stronger on the earth steadier
on our feet or they'll take us
and put us all in the sack
— one after the other
each silk sock each shadow light and air
everything that makes the earth green
and the sky blue
small houses small countries small messages
and small letters bees
and ants and earthworms
don't blow away —
stay put.
Watch out
for your heads.
Don't lose your grip. Remember
that the earth spins
round and round
and round and round
and that everything that is
comes again
— me too. Said God.

Epilog

Til en radering: «Aurora», av Anne Lise Knoff

Sol-nære, sol-fjerne,
førerløst i rommet går jorden
tungtlastet med barn og fugler,
skog-snar, sky-flekker og glassklare vinder
uten lyd og bak avstander
ennu skjønnere enn nattens
tåkeslør over hav-tummel. Barbados'
kyster eller Hebridenes.

Der de alltid motstridende
tiders meninger, protesttog, halvoppfylte
og aldri eller noenlunde bønnhørte
løper ut i sanden, våre håp
reddes fra flamme-ovnene og
knuses igjen i sutrende dagsbehov.
Til de reiser seg sky-flammende
mot Andromeda og Arcturus
og morgenen samler sine roser
kanskje bak døden, marmorhvit.
— For noen tror på håpet
stikk imot all forstand,
livet i dødens rom, dets
trossige stjerne.

Epilogue

For an etching: "Aurora," by Anne Lise Knoff

Sun-approaching, sun-departing,
pilotless in space the world goes
heavily laden with children and birds,
forest thickets, cloud patches and winds clear as glass
soundless and beyond expanses
even more beautiful than the night's
veil of mist over sea-swell. The coasts of
Barbados or the Hebrides.

Where the always conflicting
opinions of the times, the half-successful protest marches,
the never or partly granted prayers
come to nothing, where our hopes
are saved from the flaming ovens and
ground down again in whining daily needs.
Until they rise up sky-blazing
toward Andromeda and Arcturus
and the morning gathers its roses
perhaps beyond death, marble-white.
— For some believe in hope
against all reason,
in life amid death's space, in its
obstinate star.

fra PUSTEØVELSE

✳ ✳ ✳ ✳ ✳

1975

from BREATHING EXERCISE

✳ ✳ ✳ ✳ ✳

1975

Hus av glass

De ynker seg litt de gamle husene når de faller.
Knark sier det når ytterveggen går.
Blupp sier det når kjøkkenvasken ramler ned i kjelleren
og krisj krasj sier det når stuegulvet sprekker.

Men så slipper regndråpene til der putesvetten var
og sengeknirket var og hvor alle ordene ble sagt,
nytt kaldt regn som vasker bort alle riftene i luften,
nervespenningen og de onde ordene og hjertedunket
som sitter fast i luften som en hinne, et hus av glass.

Det er så greit med gamle hus,
de er ikke skrevet ned noe sted,
kan bare brettes sammen som en avis,
som et vift i luften, kyss som begge har glemt,
sorgene fra i går.

The Glass House

The old houses groan a little when they fall.
"Knark" they say when the outer wall goes.
"Bloop" says the kitchen sink when it crashes down into the
  basement
and "Crish crash" says the living-room floor when it splits.

But then the raindrops get a chance where sweat lay on the
  pillow
and the bed creaked and where all the words were said,
cold new rain that washes away all the rifts in the air,
the nervous tension and the malicious words and the
  heartbeats
that get stuck in the air like a membrane, a glass house.

How convenient old houses are,
they're not written down anywhere,
can just be folded up like a newspaper,
like a waft of air, kisses that both people have forgotten,
yesterday's sorrows.

Antenneskog

Oppe på byenes tak er det store sletter.
Dit krøp stillheten opp da det ikke var plass til den på
    gatene.
Nå kommer skogen efter.
Den må være der hvor stillheten holder til.
Tre følger på tre i underlige lunder.
Den får det ikke riktig til for bunnen er for hard.
Det blir en glissen skog, en gren mot øst,
og en mot vest. Til det ligner på kors. En skog
av kors. Og vinden spør
— Hvem hviler her
i disse dype graver?

Antenna-Forest

Up on the city's roofs there are large fields.
That's where silence crept up to
when there was no room for it on the streets.
Now the forest comes in its turn.
It needs to be where silence lives.
Tree upon tree in strange groves.
They don't really manage, because the floor is too hard.
It's a sparse forest, one branch toward the east,
and one toward the west. Until it looks like crosses. A forest
of crosses. And the wind asks
— Who's resting here
in these deep graves?

Avaldsnes

Gamle stentårn når natten faller på
kan ligne stubbene efter digre trær.
Vi kom til Avaldsnes en aften og fikk se
en gammel kirke mørkne på sin haug,
innvevd i hvite tåkeflor, en gråstensklump
som lignet mest på roten til et tre,
en kjempe-eik, en ask som engang har ruvet her
med fuglesang og med grenene spredt ut
over et hardbygd, underlig land.
Kanskje en Yggdrasil, kanskje et stridere tre,
nedblåst i tidenes vind
da grenene ble for tunge
og stormen kanskje for svær,
men hvor fløy fuglene hen,
hvor ble sangene av,
si meg det?

Avaldsnes

Old stone towers at nightfall
can resemble the stumps of giant trees.
We came to Avaldsnes one evening and saw
an old church grow dark on its hill,
woven into a white veil of mist: a granite clump
that looked like the root of a tree,
a mighty oak or ash that once loomed here
with birdsong and with branches spread out
above a rugged, mysterious land.
Perhaps an Yggdrasil, perhaps a tougher tree,
blown down in the wind of the ages
when the branches got too heavy
and the storm perhaps too severe;
but where did the birds fly off to,
what became of their songs,
can you tell me that?

Små byer i Auvergne

De små byene i Auvergne
oppe på hvert sitt fjell og under hver sin sky
ligger stille og samler støv
og samler tid.
De samler år som biene samler honning
og gjemmer dem bort på sine loft og i kjølige hvelv.
De har tårn som ligner knyttede never
og murer av glemt sol
de små byene i Auvergne,
brune som kobberstikk
mørkner de inn i natten og lysner mot neste dag.
De har små torv som blusser opp som roser
og smale gater som kommer ut av mørket og vil holde deg i
    hånden
og følge deg frem til kirken St. Hippolyte
hvor Josef og Maria står tause på sine sokler
og stirrer med stive øyne ut over et stengrått land,
om noe hjelper.

De små byene i Auvergne
(og i Dordogne og Tarn og Puy-de-Dôme)
hvor det lukter myrjord og sau og vissent løv
og elvene gjemmer seg bort i trange daler
og hvor solen oser av vin og søler den ut på skyene
— dit kommer stjernene om natten og drysser sine saltkorn,
de bitre, over berg og bakker
og de små byene i Auvergne — at de skal holde seg karske
og stille
ennå en tid.

Old Cities in Auvergne

The old cities of Auvergne
each one up on its own mountain and under its own cloud
lie still and gather dust
and gather time.
They collect years as the bees collect honey
and hide them away in their attics and in cool vaults.
They have towers that look like clenched fists
and walls of forgotten sun,
the old cities of Auvergne;
brown as copperplate prints
they darken into the night and brighten toward the next day.
They have small markets that blaze up like roses
and narrow streets that emerge from the dark and want to
        hold your hand
and lead you to the Church of St. Hippolyte
where Joseph and Mary stand silent on their pedestals
and stare out across a stone-gray land with stiff eyes
to see if anything will help.

The old cities of Auvergne
(and of Dordogne and Tarn and Puy-de-Dôme)
where it smells of bog and sheep and withered leaves
and the rivers hide themselves away in narrow valleys
and where the sun reeks of wine and spills it onto the clouds
— the stars come there at night and sprinkle their bitter
        grains of salt
over mountains and hillsides
and the old cities of Auvergne — so they will stay hardy
and still
a while longer.

Hallingskeid

Ut og inn av tunnellene,
tilslutt en som er lang nok
til at du kan speile ansiktet ditt i fjellveggen
midt mellom såpeannonsene og banksparingen
og tenke over ditt liv og dine forsømmelser,
til lyset kommer igjen som en smerte mot øynene
og forteller at du er inne i en annen dal
enn hva du trodde først og bak et annet fjell,
helt anderledes enn det du hadde tenkt,
eftersom alt med økende hast forvandles
til det motsatte av hva vi venter på,
til baksider, ur og stenrøys, ødsligheter
av verdensdimensjoner, månelandskaper
er det vi ser bre seg ut ved Reinunga og Såta,
isglitrende breer som siler ned i en dal, dypt,
svimlende glaner vi ned gjennom skyene, plutselig et hus,
dukkesmått, for mennesker, veier som sytråd,
et utsnitt av levende bindevev mens hjulene her,
tamtaratam-tamtaratam, smatrer som mitraljøseild
og vognen sover, hodene nikker i takt
bak avisoverskrifter og bilder av fjerne katastrofer
og lyset slukkes og kommer igjen
som solgitre og skyggehuller, vi er flyttet
over i ennu en dal, tåkelagt
og med glimt av is
som en ny slags jord, en ny slags frykt,
en ny slags undring og fortapelse,
— litt sent nå, kan du si, å våkne opp
til nye avsindige morgener og kjøpe nye billetter
og stige av på en stasjon hvor ingenting er kjent
og alle snur seg efter deg med trette øyne
— er han en av våre eller skal vi hate ham

Hallingskeid

In and out of the tunnels
finally one that is long enough
so you can see your face mirrored in the wall of rock
right between the soap ads and the savings plans
and can think over your life and your failures,
until the light returns like a pain to your eyes
and tells you that you are in a different valley
than you thought at first and behind a different mountain,
completely unlike what you had thought,
since everything is transformed at increasing speed
into the opposite of what we expect,
into back sides, scree and stone-piles,
wastelands on a planetary scale, moonscapes
are what we watch spreading out near Reinunga and Såta,
ice-sparkling glaciers that pour deep into a valley;
dizzily we gaze down through the clouds, suddenly a house,
as small as for dolls, but for people, roads like thread,
a band of living tissue while here the wheels,
tomtaratom-tomtaratom, rattle like machine-gun fire
and the railway car sleeps, the heads nod in rhythm
behind newspaper headlines and pictures of distant
  catastrophes
and the light is shut off and comes back
in sun-grilles and shadow-holes, we have moved
over into yet another valley, obscured by mist
and with a flash of ice
like a new kind of earth, a new kind of fear,
a new kind of awe and doom
— a little late now, you may say, to wake up
to new crazy mornings and buy new tickets
and get off at a station where nothing is familiar
and everyone follows you with tired eyes
— is he one of ours or shall we hate him

her i vår nye verden av kraftmaster og stenblokker
og hvor det mørkner og lysner vekselvis i skift
som om de ennu ikke har bestemt seg, skjønt nu haster det
for vi nærmer oss vannskillet, minutt for minutt
stiger vi stadig oppover mellom ustanselige fjell,
ut og inn gjennom mørket til bremsene skriker
inne i en ny natt, vi ser
en lykt som svinger, lys i et nakent vindu,
et pift under sneoverbygget. Vi står i mørket.
Lydløst. Hva venter vi på.
Og hvor lenge.

here in our new world of power lines and stone blocks
where it gets dark and light alternately in shifts
as if they still haven't decided, though now it's urgent
for we're coming to the divide, minute by minute
we climb steadily upward between unending mountains,
in and out through the darkness until the brakes screech
inside a new night, we see
a lantern swinging, light in a bare window, hear
a whistle under the snow shelter. We wait in the darkness.
Silently. What are we waiting for.
And for how long.

Blinde ord

— er ord som elskere sier med sin hud
inne i nattens rom hvor ingen tanker har form.

— er ord som den døende former i sin strupe
og aldri får sagt før lysene er brent ned.

— er ord som fosteret sier når det drømmer
om lyder det ikke kan høre og farver det ikke vet.

— er ord som vinden sier til treet og sorgene
til vårt hjerte.

— ord som var her før ordene ble til,
som jorden er gjort av
og som stjernene sender ut som lys
i tidløse åndedrag.

Blind Words

— are words that lovers say with their skin
inside night's space, where thoughts are without form.

— are words the dying person forms in his throat
and never gets said before the candles have burned down.

— are words the fetus says when it dreams
about sounds it cannot hear and colors it doesn't know.

— are words the wind says to the tree and sorrows
say to our heart.

— words that were here before words were created,
words that the earth is made of
and that the stars exhale as light
in their timeless breathing.

Sand

Det finnes et nøyaktig tall for alle sandkorn på jorden
såvelsom for stjerneverdnene over våre hoder,
(Det skal være like mange) hvis vi bare hadde kjent det,
men av større betydning er det å vite at sandkornene
blir stadig flere og ørknene større. Et stenk
av fiolett har blandet seg i solnedgangenes rosa.

Sand er hvit som melk og myk
som et strøk av fioliner.
Sand kysser foten din
og risler over håndflatene som rent vann.
Ved Bir el Daharrem er berg og daler gjort av bronce.
Ved Theben og Asmara ligger døde byer under sanden.

Sand er knuste fjell og asken efter alt som har vært.
Sandfluktene går over hete land som striper av ild.
Sand dekker klodene. Månestrålene er gjenskinn i sand.
Sand er det siste på jorden.
Sovende tid.

Sand

There is a precise total for all the grains of sand on earth,
as well as for the starry worlds above our heads
(supposedly the same for each), if only we knew it,
but it's more important to know that the grains of sand
grow constantly in number and the deserts are getting bigger.
  A touch
of violet has mixed itself into the pink of sunset.

Sand is white as milk and soft
as a bowing of violins.
Sand kisses your foot
and trickles over your palms like clean water.
At Bir el Daharrem hills and valleys are made of bronze.
At Thebes and Asmara dead cities lie under the sand.

Sand is crushed mountains and the ashes of everything that
    has existed.
The sand dunes cross hot countries like stripes of fire.
Sand covers the planets. Moonbeams are reflections in sand.
Sand is the last thing on earth.
Time sleeping.

Uten en lyd

Lydløsheten inne i alt som hender.
Det stummes tyngde. Lyset
som faller på et ansikt
som forandringer, ikke som fred.

Noen står der og vet ikke at de er til.
Lyder faller til jorden. Regn
splintres som glass.

Det umåtelige har ingen stemme.
Det som betyr noe. Ikke nattemørket.
Ikke sollyset. Ikke døden.

Without a Sound

The silence within everything that happens.
The weight of the unspoken. The light
that falls on a face
like changes, not like peace.

Some people stand there and don't know they exist.
Sounds fall to the earth. Rain
shatters like glass.

What is intense has no voice.
Whatever means something. Not the dark of night.
Not the sunlight. Not death.

I bringebærtiden

I bringebærtiden
kommer vepsene inn i huset,
og finner ikke ut igjen, dag efter dag
dasker de mot rutene, summe-summe-summ
til vi kan feie dem ut på søplebrettet.

Også for deg og meg
er det stengsler vi ikke kan forstå.
Vi kaster oss gang efter gang mot noe vi ikke kan se
til de feier oss ut en dag på søplebrettet.
Om ikke noen på jorderik eller i skyene
tilfeldigvis
skulle sette opp et vindu så vi kommer igjennom.

In Raspberry Season

In raspberry season
the wasps come into the house
and don't find their way out again; day after day
they dash against the windowpanes, sooma-sooma-soom
until we can sweep them out on the dustpan.

For you and me too
there are barriers we can't understand.
Time after time we throw ourselves against something
        we cannot see
until they sweep us out one day on the dustpan.
Unless, by chance,
someone on this earth or in the clouds
raises a window so we get through.

Ovenfra, nedenfra og
fra siden

Fuglesløret om jorden kan ikke sees fra satellittene
men er der allikevel som et fjærlett dirr av vingeslag,
små hamrende hjerter og lynskarpe øyenpar
fotograferer vår hverdag som spionsondene, men de
   sladrer ikke.
Nattergalen gjemmer på en sorg.

Sett fra siden ser du tingene bedre. Alt får profil.
Smør og ost. De hule kinnene. De innsunkne øynene.
Skyene er deroppe som hierarkier av dikt og drøm.
Hvorfor skjelver du på hånden?

Sett underfra er allting stort. Som hos gudene.
Metemarken tror det tordner når du setter tåen ned.
Fra den dødes synspunkt er det du som er i himlen.

From Above, from Below and from the Side

The veil of birds around the earth can not be seen from the
     satellites
but is there just the same, as a feather-light tremor of beating
     wings;
small hammering hearts and lightning-sharp double lenses
photograph our days like the orbiting spies, but they don't
     tell.
The nightingale cherishes a sorrow.

From the side you see things better. Everything acquires
     contours.
Butter and cheese. The hollow cheeks. The sunken eyes.
The clouds above are like hierarchies of poetry and dream.
Why is your hand trembling?

Seen from underneath everything is large. As among the
     gods.
The earthworm thinks it's thundering when you put your
     toe down.
From the dead's point of view, it's you who are in heaven.

Stenhistorien

— er sent fortalt
for det er så mye av den
og så tungt

som Babels murer
og ingen som kan si oss navn
på dem som tok fjellene ned
og satte dem opp igjen som festninger,
fangehull og tårn.

Verden er stiv av herrer
og tung av keiserslott.
Murene ligger igjen efter dem som skorper,
stenbruddene som arr.

For dødsfrykten er overalt
og herreveldene er overalt
og menneskehjertene holder aldri opp å slå
— hammer mot sten, hammer mot sten
så lenge tiden er til.

The History of Stone

— is late in being told
because there is so much of it
and it's so heavy

like Babel's walls
and there is no one who can tell us the names
of those who took down the mountains
and put them up again as fortresses,
dungeons and towers.

The world is stiff with masters
and heavy with the palaces of czars.
The walls are left behind like crusts,
the quarries like scars.

For the fear of death is everywhere
and the dominions of masters are everywhere
and human hearts never stop beating
— hammer on stone, hammer on stone
as long as time goes on.

Vi som bor ved jernbanen

Dagene går. Og eftersom alt får litt mindre glans
fordi det gjentar seg og gjentar seg som avisoppslagene
og ruteboken, er det mye som kan sjaltes ut som mindre
maktpåliggende såsom brevandringer i tørrsne
eller innkjøp av farvefjernsyn.
Men ikke togene. Ikke for meg.
Jeg mener tog som nabo. Hengende over havegjerdet.
Og tog langt inni tinningene. Som jordskjelv.

Jeg er bofast ved en bane. (Utsikt til en sjø)
Har skinnene utenfor veggen. (Solnedgangene er vakre her)
Og som sagt tog.

Nok av dem.
Under vinduet nattetid 2,55, 3,20 og 3,55
som billedserier, filmstriper, fragmenter
av andres liv, dertil nattoget 5,15
med sne på takene, frisk fra Dovrefjell.

Alt går over. Og fort.
Blåser det en vind mot øst, stormer det straks
mot vest. Og omvendt for at verden alltid
skal befinne seg i balanse
og ikke styrte sammen over malmtoget
som løfter deg opp av dynene 3,35
og ber deg om å Huske-huske-huske-huske
at du lever på en vulkan.

Ens posisjon blir derfor lett: betrakterens.
Alt går over. Sitte og se.
Strømninger i tiden. Ufred og godt vær.

We Who Live near the Railway

The days go by. And since everything loses a little luster
because it repeats itself and repeats itself like the
     newspaper headlines
and the timetables, there's a lot that can be dropped as less
pressing, for example hikes on glaciers in dry snow
or buying a color television.
But not the trains. Not for me.
I mean trains as neighbors. Leaning over the garden fence.
And trains deep in my temples. Like earthquakes.

I make my home near a railroad. (View of a lake)
Have the rails just outside the wall. (Sunsets are pretty here)
And, as I said, trains.

Enough of them.
Under the window at 2:55, 3:20 and 3:55 a.m.
like the comics, strips of film, fragments
of other people's lives, and then the night train at 5:15
with snow on the car-roofs, fresh from the Dovre Mountains.

Everything passes. And fast.
If a wind blows toward the east, there's soon a storm
in the west. And vice versa, so the world
will always be in balance
and won't cave in on top of the ore train
that raises you from the eiderdowns at 3:35
to insist-insist-insist-insist
that you're living on a volcano.

So one's position easily becomes the observer's.
Everything passes. Sit and watch.
Currents in time. Unrest and good weather.

Kvinneår, oljeproblemer og flom
i Gudbrandsdalslågen.

Fire kilometer hver natt, bare av gods,
for ikke å snakke om dagens
tredobbelte ekspresser. Jeg kan se
et bånd av ansikter blekne bak avisene
som lynblinkene i august. Tordenen kommer efterpå.
Alt blir en vane. Hold munn og lukk vinduene.
Og så kommer stillheten.

Det varte ikke så lenge som jeg trodde.
Årene går, pendelen svinger, den er av jern
og tung: Syd-nord, tikk-takk, nord-syd. Sitte og se
at alt går over. Til tiden er inne
for nattoget, hvis det holder ruten.
Jeg hører det alt,
først som et stille piano-pianissimo, tam-tarratam.
Derefter sterkere, som et drønn. Her har vi det
nattsvart og med tause vinduer, vogn efter vogn,
åtte boggier i natt og snefaner mellom koblingene
friske fra Fokkstumyrene og Hjerkinnhø.

Women's Year, oil problems, and flood
in Gudbrandsdalen.

Four kilometers every night, just of freight,
not to mention the day's
extra-long expresses. I can see
a band of faces behind their newspapers, flashing by
as pale as lightning in August. The thunder comes
        afterwards.
Everything becomes a habit. Shut up and close the windows.
And then comes the silence.

It didn't last as long as I thought.
The years go, the pendulum swings, it is iron
and heavy: South-north, tick-tock, north-south. Sit and watch
how everything passes. Until it's time
for the night train, if it's on schedule.
I hear it already,
at first as a quiet piano-pianissimo, tom-tarratom.
After that stronger, like a booming. Here it is,
night-black and with silent windows, car after car,
eight sleepers tonight and banners of snow between the
        couplers
fresh from the Fokkstu Bogs and the Hjerkinn Dome.

fra Tᴇɴᴋ ᴘÅ ɴᴏᴇ ᴀɴɴᴇᴛ

❋   ❋   ❋   ❋   ❋

1979

from THINK ABOUT SOMETHING ELSE

✳   ✳   ✳   ✳   ✳

1979

Fasten your seatbelts —

Å sitte fastklemt, med knærne under haken,
høyt over tordenværene og ripsbuskene,
slik ble vår skjebne når vi vil til de fjerne kyster.
Et lite glimt av Irland, moseskimlet
som i et velbrukt atlas, lynsnart
trekker de ullteppet over det igjen,
så vi skal skånes for å se det hele.
Og under det store teppet, grått efter mye vask
ligger også havet,
vannstjernen Jordens rynkede hud
som heller ikke liker for mange blikk.

Og så
kom natten,
med Jupiter, Andromeda og Sirius.
Og den som ved et tilfelle fikk vindusplassen
kan se ut på mørket, se galaxer, tåkefjerne
melkeveisystemer, verdensrommets urfjærer
som får hjertene til å tikke og gå,
tikk-takk, tikk-takk inne i alt av liv,
alt som beveger seg. På alle kloder.
Mennesker, elefanter, selv i sølvrevens trange bur
tikker det og går, hamrer det og går,
i redsel eller trygghet, elskov eller hat.
Også her, hos de 139 levende liv
15 000 fot over Atlanteren og bare 60
sjømil øst av Labrador
inne i et svevende rom som ligner en teatersalong

hvor publikum er sovnet under forestillingen,
til en liten sitring i skroget
får hjertene til å banke fortere igjen,
tikk-tikk-takk, men bare fremover, fremover

Fasten Your Seatbelts —

To sit squeezed tight, with your knees up to your chin,
high above the thunderstorms and the currant bushes,
such is our fate when we set out for distant shores.
A glimpse of moss-like Ireland, mottled
as in a well-worn atlas, and quick as lightning
they pull the wool blanket over it again,
so we'll be saved the trouble of seeing all of it.
And under the vast blanket, gray after many washings,
lies the sea as well,
Earth-the-water-star's wrinkled skin,
which also avoids our stares.

And then
comes the night,
with Jupiter, Andromeda and Sirius.
And whoever by chance has the window seat
can look out at the dark, see galaxies, distant cloudy
milky ways, outer space's mainsprings
that make the heart tick and go,
tick-tock, tick-tock within everything living,
everything that moves. On all planets.
People, elephants, even in the silver fox's narrow cage
it ticks and goes, it pounds and goes,
in terror or safety, love or hate.
Here too, in the 139 living beings
15,000 feet above the Atlantic and only 60
nautical miles east of Labrador
inside a floating room that's like a theater lounge

where the audience has dozed off during the performance,
until a slight vibration in the fuselage
sets the hearts beating faster again,
tick-tick-tock, but only forward, forward

i et liv som ingen av oss vet slutten på,
eftersom hvert sekund du lever
er som spissen på en pil — din egen tid,
der du alt er blitt eldre efter første linje i diktet.
Så du må gjerne bla om. Men reis deg ikke og gå,
for vi er fremme snart
i den nye tiden, der snart alt er gjort av glass
og gjennomsiktig, for vi har fått nye øyne
og hårde. Du ser nesten alt som hender på Jorden.
Og gleden din blir langsomt dempet ned.

No smoking allowed.
Please fasten your seatbelts.
Og så ned på jorden, til regnværet,
rulletrappene og drosjekøene.
Det er livet ditt
jeg skriver om.

in a life none of us knows the conclusion of,
since each second you live
is like the point of an arrow — your own time —
where you've already gotten older after the first line in the
        poem.
So by all means turn the page. But don't get up and leave,
because we'll be arriving soon
in the new era, where everything will soon be made of glass,
transparent, for we've acquired new eyes,
hard ones. You see almost everything that happens on Earth.
And your delight gets slowly subdued.

No smoking allowed.
Please fasten your seatbelts.
And then the landing, down to the rain,
the escalators and the waiting-lines for taxis.
It is your life
I'm writing about.

Bildene

— har det lettvint nå.
Får gå rett inn i stua,
sofaen og den beste stolen.
Ordene
har fått lengre vei å gå,
kanskje må de hvile litt også,
kjemme håret eller tørke av skoene,
(det et litt sølete ofte)
så får de komme inn i stua, de også,
men ikke i sofaen.

The Images

—have it easy now.
Make themselves at home,
get the sofa and the best chair.
The words
have to take the long way around,
maybe they have to rest a while too,
comb their hair or clean off their shoes
(often the road's a bit muddy);
then they can come in too,
but they don't get the sofa.

Mediadiktet

Alt dette vi skal stappe inn i øynene våre nå.
Alle farvenes lyn og tordenvær, angstrop og skrik.
Trykksvertestrømmenes evige Niagara. Hver dag — hver dag.
Nilfloder av halvtenkte tanker. Følg med. Gi plass.
Press det sammen for det kommer mer. Hiv ut det gamle.
Ut med det. Det nye er viktigere. Hold takt
med tiden. Og den er NÅ.

Stapp det inn i øynene. Dytt på her. Inn med det.
Klem det sammen til forte slagord. Ingen plass mer
til lange forklaringer — eftertanker —. Hiv det ut.
Du har fått enda ett øye nå, vet du,
så nå ser du hele verden — eller nesten.
(Det blir i allfall pene farver på det — kanskje ikke helt,
men bortimot.)

Å se det meste, vite nesten alt
kunne bare Vårherre (i sin tid).
Men var han glad for det? Det sa de ikke noe om.
For vi som lever nå blir aldri riktig glade mer.
Ikke som ungene, eller som liljene på marken, lerkesangen.
For det vi har sett og hørt går aldri bort igjen.
Torden og lyn. Vi fullstappes dag efter dag
som fra foringsmaskiner for broilerhjerner, tettpakket
i våre bur. — Det er bare å gape, så kommer det.
Og ingen har lov å unnslå seg. Du har å sitte der.

— — —

The Media Poem

All this we're supposed to stuff into our eyes now.
All the colors' lightning and thunder, cries of anguish and
    screams.
An endless Niagara of printer's ink. Every day — every day.
Flooding Niles of half-formed thoughts. Keep up. Make
    room.
Cram it in, there's more on the way. Throw out what's old.
Out with it. What's new is more important. Keep pace
with the times. And that means NOW.

Stuff it into your eyes. Shove it in here. In with it.
Squeeze it into quick slogans. No more room
for long explanations — reflections —. Throw that out.
You've gotten a third eye now, you know,
so now you see the whole world — or almost.
(It's got pretty colors, at any rate — maybe not perfect,
but close to it.)

To see and know almost everything —
only Our Lord could do that (in his day).
But did it make him happy? They didn't comment on that.
For we who live now are never really happy anymore.
Not like children, or the lilies in the field, the
    lark-song.
For what we have seen and heard never goes away again.
Thunder and lightning. We're stuffed full day after day
as if by feeding-machines for brains like chickens, packed
    tight
in our coops. — Just open wide and it comes.
And no one is allowed to refuse. Your job is to sit there.

— — —

Idag er det blåsevær ute. Hele Mjøsa er hvit.
Sitte og se her på sneen og vinden
som skriver på den med usynlig blekk.
Puste en liten stund. Men ikke for lenge. Glad
får du lov til å bli. Men bare for små, små ting.
Og røm ikke tilskogs. Vi finner deg.

Men ennå har vi jo lov å tenke (mens øynene tygger og
    svelger)
at det er noe de gjemmer for oss. Noe de ikke vet ennå.
Bortenfor lydene og lyset. Sannheter
utenfor sannhetene.
Sånne som vinden skriver på sneen. For under sneen ligger
    jorden
og venter. Full av groe. Full av håp. Vet den mer
enn vi?

It's windy out today. Lake Mjøsa is all white.
Sit here and watch the snow, and the wind
writing on it with invisible ink.
Breathe for a while. But not for too long. You have
    permission
to be happy. But only for little, little things.
And don't run away to the woods. We'll find you.

But in fact we can still manage to think (while our eyes chew
    and swallow)
that there's something they're hiding from us. Something they
    don't know yet.
Beyond the sounds and the light. Truths
beyond the truths.
Like the ones the wind writes on the snow. For under the
    snow the earth
lies waiting. Full of sprouts. Full of hope. Does it know
more than we do?

Kom igjen —

Dypt derinne,
bakenfor det tunge kneet mitt idag,
ligger et annet lite kne,
litt skittent og med skrubbsår på.
Og inne i fingrene mine, alle fem,
ligger en liten hånd, en annen,
ennå litt engstelig, men varm.
Og langt inne i skallen min,
helt innerst der,
kribler det av andre tanker,
rare og små, nesten med hyssing rundt, men de puster
ennå. Fulle av forventning, nesten av fryd.
Det hender det klør i dem —
de vil ut og leke
gjemsel med meg. Ofte — ofte.
Men da er de borte plutselig. Jeg finner
dem ikke igjen. Det er gått så mange år,
og blitt så mange svære lag av tid
utenpå alt.
— — — Men kom igjen da dere. Kom igjen,
så løper vi og gjemmer oss
alle, alle.

Come Back —

Deep inside,
behind that heavy knee I've got today,
lies another, smaller knee,
a little dirty, and scraped.
And within my fingers, all five of them,
lies a small hand, another one,
still a bit anxious, but warm.
And far inside my skull,
in the innermost part,
other thoughts are tingling,
odd and small ones, almost wrapped up tight, but
        they're still
breathing. Full expectation, almost of joy.
Sometimes they itch —
they want to come out and play
hide-and-seek with me. Often — often.
But then they are suddenly gone. I can't
find them again. So many years have passed,
so many heavy layers of time
have settled over everything.
— — — But come back anyway, all of you. Come back,
and we'll run and hide,
every one, every one.

Se opp (OBS. OBS.)

Blir det sol på søndag?
Paraply på værkartet?
Vel, vel. Ditt problem.

Mitt er av et annet slag.
Kikk litt opp på skyene (engang du får tid).
De hører med til familien. Bor i annen etasje.
Og vi i første. Samme hus.

Og samme spørsmål. Noen
må ut og skure og vaske. Ofte natten lang.
Hustak og gater. Vanner rosenbed og dusjer
plenene til gartneren.
Noen dovner seg i solen. The Jet Set,
på luftmadrasser. Andre
bygger seg luksusboliger,
finere enn Ullernåsen. Hele slott
med tårn og takterrasser, swimmingpools
som provoserer til kanonbrak. Tordenbyger.
Glimt av ild,
til vinden rolig soper bort det hele.

Og noen blir trøtte av verden. Kei av alt.
Legger seg ned for å sove oppe i åsene.
Deprimerte. Ofte i dagevis.
Helt til solen kommer stikkende med sin sprøytespiss.
Da rusler de.

Og så har vi tåken. Skyene som tviler,
og går ned i gatene for å finne sannheten der.
Gjør de det?

Faktisk holder jeg meg mest til duskregnet
— sånn i det lange løp. Regnvær

Look Up (N.B. N.B.)

Will it be sunny on Sunday?
Umbrella on the weather map?
Well, then. Your problem.

Mine's of a different sort.
Take a peek up at the clouds (whenever you have time).
They're part of the family. Live on the second floor.
And we're on the first. Same house.

And the same question. Somebody
has to go out and scrub and wash. Often all night.
Roofs and streets. Water rosebeds and sprinkle
the gardener's lawns.
Some loaf in the sun. The Jet Set,
on air mattresses. Others
build luxurious villas for themselves,
finer than in Ullernåsen. Whole castles —
with towers and roof patios, swimming pools —
that provoke the crash of cannons. Thundershowers.
Flashes of fire
until the wind calmly sweeps it all away.

And some get tired of the world. Fed up with everything.
Lie down to sleep up in the hills.
Depressed. Often for days at a time.
Until the sun comes pricking with its hypodermic.
That rouses them.

And then we have the fog. Clouds that are in doubt
and go down into the streets to find the truth there.
Do they find it?

The fact is, I stick mostly to the drizzly days
— I mean for the long haul. Rainy weather

233

er godt å jobbe i (for den som er innendørs).
Og det gjør jobben sin bra.
Vasker vinduet og utgangsdøren. Hele gaten.
Og gir gro-vann over alt det grønne. Hele jorden.
Alt det som vokser. Skogens trær og rug og ris og hvete.
Så jeg holder meg til det som ikke blender.
Skyslott og silkehimler. Pent å se på.
Men det holder ikke.
Gråværet
kan du stole på.

is good to work in (if you work indoors).
And it does its job well.
Washes the windows and the front door. The whole street.
And waters all the greenery. The whole earth.
Everything that grows. The trees in the forest and rye and
  rice and wheat.
So I stick to what isn't dazzling.
Cloud-castles and silky skies. Nice to look at.
But that's not enough.
Gray weather
is the kind you can trust.

Du fugl —

Du fugl i meg
— jeg kjenner vingen din.
Jeg kjenner nebbet hakke — hakke
mot sprinklene i brystet mitt. Jeg vet
du er en fange her.
Men vent
en liten stund.
Bare en liten stund,
så er du fri,
du fugl i meg.

You Bird —

You bird in me
— I feel your wing.
I feel your beak pecking — pecking
against the bars in my breast. I know
you are a prisoner here.
But wait
a little while.
Just a little while,
then you'll be free,
you bird in me.

Til deg

Tiden går (hva skal den ellers ta seg til).
En dag hører du den banke på døren din.
Den har banket på hos oss,
men jeg lukket ikke opp.
Ikke dennegang.

Vet du,
jeg har ofte stått og sett litt på deg,
sånn om morgenen foran speilet der
når du kjemmer håret ditt, det
knitrer i det, som i sne i påskefjellet
og du bøyer deg litt frem (jeg ser det godt)
— er det kommet en rynke til?
— Det er det ikke. For meg
er du ung.
Det er sevje i deg, skog. Et tre

og med fugler i. De synger enda.
Kanskje litt lavt i høst, men likevel.
— Ikke en dag uten en latter i strupen,
eller det sakte streifet av en hånd.

En gang
må jeg holde den enda fastere,
for du vet, vi skal ut og reise snart,
og ikke med samme båt.
Noen har banket på døren vår, men gått igjen.
Dette
er visst det eneste vi aldri
har villet snakke om.

To You

Time moves along (what else would it be up to).
One day you hear it knocking on your door.
It has knocked at our place,
but I didn't open up.
Not this time.

You know,
I've often stopped for a bit and watched you,
like in the morning in front of the mirror there
when you comb your hair, it
crackles, like snow in the mountains at Easter
and you bend forward a little (I see it clearly)
— I think that's another wrinkle.
— No it isn't. For me
you are young.
There is sap in you, forest. A tree

with birds in it. They still sing.
Perhaps a bit softly this autumn, but nonetheless.
— Not one day without a laugh in the throat
or the slow touch of a hand.

At some point
I'll have to hold it even tighter,
because, you know, we'll be traveling soon,
and not on the same boat.
Someone has knocked on our door, but gone away again.
Surely this
is the only thing we've never
wanted to talk about.

Om å sovne i en åker

Jeg kan huske jeg har sovnet i en åker, engang
da jeg var liten, fem-seks år og dum, engang,
og våknet av en frosk som satt på foten min
midt i en skog av grønnere enn grønt, engang.
Et tusenben kom krypende på hånden min,
og ør-små dyr jeg ikke kjente før, engang,
og kryp med underlige farver på
som kom og ville se hva dette var.
— En Gulliver i Lilleputters land, engang.
En snegl på kinnet mitt og maur i håret.
To markmus, de som har så blanke øyne
sto engstelig på vakt bak hvert sitt strå, engang.
Det var som i et hav, et verdensdyp, engang,
som ingen kjenner nå, men jeg fikk se, engang.
Og det jeg husker best var alt det duftet av.
— Av jord — som ligner jodlukt — og av alt som gror,
          engang.
Den stramme eim av sæd og gammel muld, engang,
og litt av kumøkk,
engang.

On Falling Asleep in a Field

I can remember falling asleep in a field, once
when I was little, five or six and dumb, once,
and being wakened by a frog that sat on my foot
in the middle of a forest greener than green, once.
A centipede came crawling onto my hand,
and tiny creatures I hadn't met before, once,
and insects colored marvelously
that came to see what this was.
— A Gulliver in a land of Lilliputians, once.
A snail on my cheek and ants in my hair.
Two field mice, the kind that have such shiny eyes,
stood anxious watch behind their blades of grass, once.
It was like being in an ocean, the depths of the world, once,
which no one knows anymore, but which I got to see, once.
And what I remember best is everything it smelled of.
— Of earth — which smells like iodine — and of everything
        that grows, once.
The pungent odor of semen and old humus, once,
and a whiff of cow dung,
once.

Bortafor Grorud —

Til Olav H. Hauge på 70-årsdagen

Det er ikke nødvendig
å bo i slike digre byer.
Det er ikke nødvendig
å rope høyt fra talerstoler
for å bli hørt.
Det er ikke nødvendig
stadig å tenke andres tanker
eller å snakke med andres munn.

Rart land, det her,
— bortafor Grorud.
Nordlys og nymåne
istedenfor gatelys.
Myrsørpe istendenfor fortauer.
Svupp — svupp sier det når du går
inn i de nye tidene, foran de fleste
som ikke kan se eller høre for motorbrølet,
neonflammene eller de skingrende stemmene.

Jeg er litt småsvak for de svære fjellene
der vest, islyset fra fonnene, og havet
som stikker fingrene inn her for å kjenne
om vi ennå er blant de levende,
— og for de store stillhetene —
(du får god hørsel av dem
og våre nerver). Du hører tingene
nesten før det er skjedd
— bortafor Grorud
eller Hakadal eller Sokna. Lese og lytte
og skrive ned. Slippe
å tenke andres tanker,
eller snakke med andres munn.

Beyond Grorud —

for Olav H. Hauge on his 70th birthday

It is not necessary
to live in such enormous cities.
It is not necessary
to shout from rostrums
in order to be heard.
It is not necessary
always to think others' thoughts
or to speak with others' mouths.

Strange country, around here,
— beyond Grorud.
Northern lights and a new moon
instead of street lights.
Marsh sludge instead of sidewalks.
Svurp-svurp it says when you walk
into the next age, ahead of the crowd,
who cannot see or hear for the roar of engines,
the neon flames or the piercing voices.

I have a weakness for those massive mountains
to the west, the icy light from the drifts, and the ocean
that sticks its fingers in here to feel
if we are still among the living,
— and for the great silences —
(you get good hearing from them,
and sharpened senses). You hear things
almost before they have happened
— beyond Grorud
or Hakadal or Sokna. Read and listen
and write it down. Escape
thinking others' thoughts,
or speaking with others' mouths.

Hundvåko

Hundvåko, Hangur og Skriulaupen.
Underlige navn vi har i dette landet vårt,
liksom hogd ut av berget, rett og slett,
eller skåret ut av gamle trestubber.

Men de svarer liksom ikke lenger til noe.
Vil kanskje ikke kjennes ved oss,
og ikke vi ved dem. Ikke motellene. Ikke bensinstasjonene,
og det vi snakker om eller tenker på.

Framrusthovdi, Uppnostindann', Tindulvstølane.
Det må ha bodd noen her før
som var mere kjente her enn vi er blitt,
og tok ordene rett ut av fjellveggen
og hogde dem til for oss som runer.
Holder det?

Hundvåko

Hundvåko, Hangur and Skriulaupen.
Peculiar names we have in this country of ours,
as if hacked out of the mountains, pure and simple,
or chipped out of old tree stumps.

But it seems like they no longer fit anything.
Perhaps they're avoiding us,
and we them. Our motels. Our gas stations,
and what we talk or think about.

Framrusthovdi, Uppnostindann', Tindulvstølane.
People must have lived here before
who were familiar with the place in a way we've lost,
and took the words right out of the rock face
and carved them for us like runes.
Will they last?

Fjellregel

Det er den tynne sneen,
den som falt inatt,
som er så farlig, sier de.
Det ligger et islag under der
av gammel, forherdet sne. Det er den
som setter de store skredene igang
— de som river med seg alle.

Nysne, tynn, sprø
er falt inatt,
så trå ikke feil.
Husk på den gamle sneen,
den seige skorpen som ligger der og venter.
Så hold unna bratthenget.
Det kan begynne som en torden
og ende som en blinkende ljå.

Mountain Rule

It's the thin snow,
the kind that fell tonight,
that's so dangerous, they say.
Underneath it there's a layer of ice
made of old, hardened snow. That's what
sets off the big avalanches
— the ones that sweep everyone away.

Fresh snow, thin, crisp
has fallen tonight,
so don't miss a step.
Remember the old snow,
the tough crust is lying there waiting.
So stay away from the steep slope.
It can start like a thunderclap
and end like a flashing scythe.

— Mere fjell

Av og til
må noe vare lenge,
ellers mister vi vel vettet snart,
så fort som allting snurrer rundt med oss.
Store trær er fint
og riktig gamle hus er fint,
men enda bedre —
fjell.
Som ikke flytter seg en tomme
om hele verden enn forandres
(og det må den snart),
så står de der
og står og står
så du har noe å legge pannen inntil,
og kjøle deg
og holde i noe fast.

Jeg trivs med fjell.
De lager horisonter
med store hugg i,
som de var smidd av smeder.
Tenk på: — Den gamle nupen her har stått som nå
helt siden Haralds-tiden.
Den sto her da de spikret en arming fast til korset.
Som nå. Som nå.
Med sildrebekker på og lyngkjerr og den store
bratte pannen
uten tanker i. Den sto her
under Belsen og Hiroshima. Den står her nå
som landemerke for din død, din uro,

— More Mountains

Here and there
something must endure,
or soon we'll surely lose our wits,
we've got everything whirling around so fast.
Large trees are fine
and really old houses are fine,
but even better —
mountains.
Which won't budge an inch
even if the whole world is changed
(as it soon must be);
they'll stand there
and stand and stand
so you can lay your forehead against something,
and cool yourself
and hold onto something solid.

I'm content in the mountains.
They make horizons
with big notches,
as if they were forged by smiths.
Think of it: — That old round-top has stood as it stands now
all the time since King Harald's day.
It stood here when they nailed a poor wretch to the cross.
As it stands now. As it stands now.
Wearing trickling streams and heather scrub and that large
steep brow
without any thoughts in it. It stood here
through Belsen and Hiroshima. It stands here now
as a landmark for your death, your unease,

kanskje dine håp.
Så du kan gå derbort og holde i noe hardt.
Noe gammelt noe. Som stjernene.
Og kjøle pannen din på den,
og tenke tanken ut.
Og tenke selv.

perhaps your hopes.
So you can go over there and hold onto something hard.
Some old something. Like the stars.
And cool your forehead on it,
and think your thoughts through.
And think for yourself.

Klokkene fra Assisi

Hør klokkeklangene fra Assisi ved morgengry.
De flyr som fugleflokker, høyt mot himlen over Umbria.
«Vi finner dem — Vi finner dem — Vi finner dem.»

Hør klokketonene fra Assisi ved aftentid,
når de som trette fugleskarer vender hjem igjen:
«Vi fant dem ikke — fant dem ikke — fant dem ikke.»

— Ikke EN som ville skjenke oss sin kappe.
— Ikke EN som ville legge ned sitt sverd.

The Bells from Assisi

Hear the peals of the bells from Assisi at daybreak.
They fly like birds, high against the heavens over Umbria.
"We'll find them — We'll find them — We'll find them."

Hear the notes of the bells from Assisi in the evening,
when like tired flocks of birds they turn back home:
"We couldn't find them — couldn't find them — couldn't
    find them."

— Not ONE who would offer us his cloak.
— Not ONE who would lay down his sword.

«*Silvery Moon*»

Hva gjør du i downtown, Kansas City (Mo.) om kvelden
når det plutselig dukker opp en diger flod foran øynene dine
med en bru av måneskinn tvers over møkkavannet, nesten
    som
Hollywood, og du sitter på en støpejernsbenk i Kersey Coates,
midt under pengetårnene?

Du blir sittende bare og kope, selvfølgelig
(og vente på at noen skal slå deg ned, eller i allefall
bomme deg for en sigarett).

Joda. Han kom. Og han fikk sin røyk.
I am an artist myself (have been), he said.
I am a painter.
Og du sitter her og myser på denne månen vår.
Slutt nå med det. We've been there, you know.
Det er bare aske og sand. Sånn som med oss.
Glitter og stas
lager vi bedre selv. Nei, sola du.
Sola. Sånn som van Gogh.
Og menneskene——
sånn som de er.
Men si meg en ting,
(Har du en blås til). Jeg har spurt meg selv
— Hvordan kan det ha seg
at vi snart vet mere om månen idag
enn om menneskene?

Ser du vestover der.
Der kommer Kansas River (Dodge City, you know it?)

"Silvery Moon"

What do you do in downtown Kansas City (Mo.) at night
when an enormous river suddenly turns up before your eyes
with a bridge of moonlight straight across the filthy water,
    almost like
Hollywood, and you're sitting on a cast-iron bench in
    Kersey Coates,
right below the money-towers?

You just keep sitting there and gaping, obviously
(and expect someone to mug you, or at least
bum a cigarette off you).

Yessir. He came. And he got his smoke.
I am an artist myself (have been), he said.
I am a painter.
And you're sitting here squinting at this moon of ours.
Well quit it. *We've been there, you know.*
It's only ashes and sand. Just like down here.
As for glitter and flash
we do that better ourselves. Nah, the sun's the thing,
    you know.
The sun. Like in Van Gogh.
And people ——
such as they are.
But tell me something
(Have you got another smoke). I've asked myself
— How is it that one of these days
we're gonna know more about the moon
than about people?

Look west there.
That's the Kansas River *(Dodge City, you know it?)*

og her kommer Missouri, bak søppeltomtene derborte.
Har du sett no så stygt som her.
To floder — mektige — som møtes.
Og så blir det dette.
— Nei, jeg får vel rusle. Jobbe litt ikveld.
Må jo leve
etpar år til iallfall, så vi får se
om det går til helvete med alt,
som noen sier.
Om du vil vite det så er jeg født i Tulsa,
Arkansas River — samme styggedommen der.

Ja, som jeg sa deg, broder.
Jeg driver og maler litt, men bare tant og flitter.
Alt sånt som smiler, — helt til øra.
Folk som er sinnssykt glade både dag og natt.
Ansikter uten rynker, juks og svindel.
Sannheten er de redd for. Tårer
selger ikke. Ikke for meg.
Det er jeg som drysser sølvpengene over elva
og lager skyer sånn som ikveld, med gullkant på.
Så nå skjønner du vel (En fyrstikk, Mister)
at det er jeg som er månen,
så nå kan du si at du så meg full
og fager i Kansas City, Terrace Park,
downtown i Kersey Coates.

and here comes the Missouri, behind those empty lots full of
    rubbish.
Ever seen a place so ugly?
Two rivers — huge ones — that meet.
And we end up with this.
— Well, I guess I'll get going. Work a little tonight.
Gotta live
a couple of more years anyway, so we can see
if everything goes up in smoke
like some people say.
In case you want to know, I was born in Tulsa,
Arkansas River — same awfulness there too.

Yeah, like I said, brother.
I do a little painting — but only worthless crap.
Everything smiling — from ear to ear.
People who're insanely happy day and night.
Faces without wrinkles, lying junk.
They're afraid of the truth. Tears
don't sell. Not for me.
I'm the one who scatters the silver coins over the river
and makes clouds like tonight, with gilt edges.
So now you understand, I guess (A match, mister)
that the moon is me,
and now you can say that you saw me lit up
and handsome in Kansas City, Terrace Park,
downtown in Kersey Coates.

257

Inlandsbanan

(Gällivare – Östersund, tog 4679)

Det går et tog for kanonenes skyld
gjennom det innerste av Skandinavia.
Jeg så bautaen over de første falne,
de som ikke sprang fort nok da mineskuddene smalt,
og det var mange. Men nesten ingen idag
stiger av eller på
ved Kåbdalis, Moskosel eller Koosakåbbå,
stasjoner som dør snart, de har ingen vinduer mer,
så her er det stopp bare for dyrene, elgerumper
i ny og ne, en tiur i sporet, og flokken av reinsdyr
som ikke vil rikke seg. De har tid nok.

For mennesket bor ikke her. «Evakuering»
sa skrivebordsfolket. Nå bor de i kjøpegatene
og stappes med leketøy så de tier.
Utdødde smågrender haster forbi. Likhauger av hus,
og en stripe av asfalt
som viser veien til kirkegården.

Men nordlyset lever ennå. Blafrende som gardiner.
Noen har åpnet et himmelvindu her. Det flagrer i blått og
        grønt
ut mot et ukjent rom. — Klar til evakuering
også her?
Nye stasjoner, halvdøde av sult:
Vargtandberget, Vojmån og Vilhelmina.
Store elver Lule, Pite og Ume
på sterke broer, spent over for troppetogenes skyld,
skjønt det sitrer i dem som hos redde soldater

The Inland Line

(Gällivare – Östersund, Sweden, train 4697)

For the sake of the cannons there is a train
that runs through the heart of Scandinavia.
I saw the rough stone monument
raised over the first to fall,
the ones who didn't run fast enough when the blasting
     charges went off,
and there were many. But today almost no one
gets on or off
at Kåbdalis, Moskosel, or Koosakåbbå,
stations that will die soon, they have no windows anymore,
so these are stops only for the animals, moose rumps
now and then, a wood grouse on the tracks, and the herd of
     reindeer
that won't budge. They have time enough.

For people don't live here. "Evacuation"
said the paper-pushers. Now they live in the shopping malls
and get drowned in toys so they'll keep quiet.
Extinct villages rush by. Mounds of cadaverous houses,
and a strip of asphalt
that shows the way to the graveyard.

But the northern lights are still alive. Fluttering like curtains.
Someone has opened a window in the sky here. Blue and
     green
flap out toward uncharted space. — Ready for evacuation
here too?
New stations, half starved to death:
Vargtandberget, Vojmån and Vilhelmina.
Across big rivers, the Lule, the Pite and the Ume,
on strong bridges, built for the troop trains
— but they tremble like frightened soldiers,

for farten er stor, 110 – 120. Ved Ulriksfors
kommer en tant ombord med kaffe och tidningar,
og med øynene stappet fulle av terror og voldtekter,
kvinnepupper og krig, kjører vi inn på Östersund Central
spor fire, 21,23 presis efter ruten.

for the speed is high, 110 – 120. At Ulriksfors
a matron comes aboard with "coffee and papers,"
and with eyes jammed full of terrorism and rapes,
women's breasts and war, we ride into Östersund Central,
track four, 9:23 p.m., exactly on time.

Notes

Some of the information in these notes has been provided by Rolf Jacobsen.

The pronunciations given here are approximations only. The system of phonetic transcription is that used in the Merriam Webster dictionaries, except that "ȯ" here stands for the pure *o* sound of French, Spanish, or German, rather than for the English *aw* sound of "hawk." A superscript "y" indicates that the tongue is held in position for initial *y* (as in "yes") while the *preceding* sound is pronounced.

Plate Glass   p. 17
"We left a blue wake behind us...." The blueness of the wavy reflections is not just the poet's fancy. There have been blue trolleys in Oslo since 1894, and blue became the color of the entire fleet within a year or two after 1924, when the municipality acquired all privately owned lines.

Railroad Country   p. 23
The Norwegian word *boggi* is taken from the British term "bogie," which denotes both a four-wheeled truck that can swivel in relation to the railroad car mounted on it, and a car mounted on such a truck. *Brekkvogn* now means "baggage car," but once referred to freight cars as well; *brekk* simply means "brake."

Hjerpetjerns-hovet \\'yar-pe-,sh^yarns-'hȯ-ve\\: a tunnel (named for the mountain it passes through) that was opened for traffic on the Southern Line of the Norwegian State Railway at about the time this poem was written.

Coke   p. 49
Oslo was known as Christiania from 1624 to 1877, and as Kristiania \\,kris-tē-'än-ē-ä\\ from 1877 to 1924, when the original name of the city on that site was restored. Teatergaten (Theater Street) is in the downtown area of the city.

Express Train   p. 55

The present Norwegian text corrects the various errors of earlier editions and embodies Rolf Jacobsen's intention that the opening part of the poem be set so as to indicate that it is prose. Division of the prose passage into two paragraphs is a new revision for this edition.

For *boggi*, see the note to "Railroad Country."

The Skarvang \'skär-,väŋ\ Hills: a fictitious place name.

Marnardal \'mär-när-,däl\: a town and railroad station in West Agder, about 20 miles (30 km) west of Kristiansand.

In the Varald Forest   p. 61

The Varald \ 'vä-,räl \ Forest is in Hedmark, on the Swedish border, about 15 miles (25 km) east of Kongsvinger and 60 miles (100 km) east of Oslo. Varildbakken, or Varild Hill, is a small settlement south of the forest.

Lebbikø \'le-bik-,ōē\, Jakobsbakken \'yä-kȯbs-,bäkᵊn\, Sarjalampi \,sär-yä-'läm-pē\, and Vais \vaēs\ all lie nearby in Finnskogene, or the Finns' Forests, an area populated by Finnish immigrants from about 1600 onwards.

The Valley of Gudbrandsdal \'gūēd-bräns-,däl\ is a large valley renowned for its beauty. It runs northwest from Lillehammer. Grip \grēp\ is a group of tiny islands in Møre and Romsdal, about 10 miles (15 km) north of Kristiansund. A lighthouse there bears the same name.

North Fosen \'fü-sᵊn\, Bykle-hei \'buɛk-le-'haē\, Kvinnegardslii \'kvin-e-,gärs-'lē-yē\, Vinje \'vin-ye\: The place names are meant to convey Norway's large extent and varied geographical character.

The Age of the Great Symphonies   p. 69

Villabyene means "the cities of private houses" and contrasts with *murstenshavet*, "the sea of brick"— older apartment buildings in the centers of cities.

"Seid umschlungen Millionen" \'zaēd ûm-'shluŋ-en mi-lē-'ȯ-nen\ is a phrase from Schiller's "An die Freude" (in English commonly known as "Ode to Joy"), the poem that provided the text for the last movement of Beethoven's Ninth Symphony (1823). It means "Be embraced, you millions."

The Archaeologist *p. 71*

The lines in Old Norse are a transcription of the first sentence of the inscription on the Eggjum Stone, Norway's most famous rune-stone, which dates from slightly before 700 A.D. They mean, approximately, "The stone is not sought by sun nor cut by knife [*or* sword]." There has been considerable debate among scholars about the sentence's exact lexical content and its intended meaning. Some, referring to well-known beliefs that exposure to sunlight and contact with iron vitiate magical powers, hold that the sentence attests to the way the inscription was made. Others read the sentence as an invocation against grave-robbers.

Blommenholm \'blȯm-en-,hȯlm\: a suburb and railway stop west of Oslo.

Timber *p. 77*

Ångermanelven, the Ångerman \ 'ȯŋ-er-män \ River, flows south and southeast across Sweden and empties into the Gulf of Bothnia (at about 63° N.) just past Kramfors, which is the center for the area's lumber-based industry.

Deep Creek, British Columbia, is the name of a small settlement 40 miles (65 km) east of Kamloops and of a river that arises nearby and flows south for about 20 miles (30 km) into Okanagan Lake.

Turnip Crop *p. 91*

Huitzilopochtli \ ,wē-tsē-lō-'pōch-tlē\ was a warrior-god, the mythic leader and chief divinity of the Aztecs. His name means "Hummingbird of the South"; he may have been a god of the southern sun. His temple, in the center of Tenochtitlan, was the object of a famous battle with Cortez and his men in 1520; it was razed after the conquest.

Stave Churches p. 95

The poem takes as its starting point the distinctive wooden churches that were built in Norway (especially the western parts of it) during the Middle Ages. The earliest surviving stave churches date from the first half of the twelfth century. The timber is often reddish brown; some of the exterior carved ornaments resemble wings or the figureheads of sailing ships.

Laudate: the verse is from Psalm 113: "Praise, O ye servants of the Lord, praise the name of the Lord."

Old Men's Graves p. 101

In accordance with Rolf Jacobsen's wishes, the present Norwegian text restores wording that appeared in editions earlier than the *Samlede dikt* of 1977.

The Foundryman of Waterfalls p. 109

The sound of a waterfall in a forest changes as one moves. Here Jacobsen imagines a mythical "man," a spirit of the waterfalls, who is responsible for their noise and their work.

In the Hall of Gobelin Tapestries p. 117

By capitalizing *Timian*, Jacobsen makes "thyme" a fictitious painter who is paired with Botticelli in an amusing, and untranslatable, figure. *Kløverknekt*, literally "clover-knave," also means the Knave (or Jack) of Clubs.

Now the River Is Carrying Off Its Lights p. 133

As the height of summer approaches, the streams dry up, and the water disappears along with its reflections.

Thoughts upon Listening In on a Radio Telescope p. 159

The reference of the Sagene \'sä-ge-ne\ trolley is a joke: Sagene is a section of Oslo just outside the downtown area; the trolley is an especially old one.

Unthinking — p. 161
In accordance with Rolf Jacobsen's wishes, the present Norwegian text restores wording that appeared in editions earlier than the *Samlede dikt* of 1977.

Waiting Time   p. 167
Oboslisten, "the Oslo Housing list": *Obos* is an acronym for *Oslo bolig- og sparelag*, or Oslo Housing and Savings Company. The wait for an apartment can take many years.

Peasant Norway   p. 169
It is not clear how far back in time the poem goes. The feudal system in Norway was brought to an end in the course of the 18th century. By 1750 a majority of farmers owned their own land. The constitution of 1814 gave power to the farmers; the nobility was abolished in 1821. On the other hand, in 1850 there were still large numbers of *husmenn*, or cotters, who did not own the land they worked and had little political power. The cotters survived, in dwindling numbers, into the present century.

Some   p. 171
Since *noen* means both "someone" and "some (people)," the changes in number are a matter of interpretation, and move through the poem more sinuously in Norwegian than in English.

Signs of Winter   p. 173
Line 2 is a free rendering based on an explanation provided by Rolf Jacobsen: "the rotting leaves give off an odor of formaldehyde." The original reads, literally, "The aspens' leaves are killed with formalin capsules."

Green Man   p. 181
A glance at the Norwegian will show how Jacobsen has managed to make the whole poem echo with the sound of barking dogs.

Angelus   p. 183

The title is the name of a devotion that commemorates the Annunciation; it is the first word of the versicle (Luke 1:28): *Angelus domini nuntiavit Mariæ*, "The angel of the Lord announced unto Mary." The quotation at the end of the first stanza, well known as part of the Magnificat, is from Luke 1:48 (see Samuel 1:11 for the Old Testament analogue).

Hva sier stjernene, "What Do the Stars Say," is a common title for astrology columns in newspapers.

Briefing   p. 185

The beginning of the poem refers to Matthew 19:14 and Mark 10:14.

Epilogue   p. 187

"Aurora" in the subtitle refers only to the dawn, not to northern lights.

Avaldsnes   p. 195

Avaldsnes \'ä-väls-,ne^{y}s\ is a point, or headland, on the west coast of Norway, just south of Haugesund, on the eastern shore of Karmøy (Karm Island).

Yggdrasil \Norw. 'ɪɛg-drä-,sēl, Engl. 'ig-drə-,sil\: in Norse mythology, the tree of the universe, a huge ash tree that binds heaven, earth, and hell together.

Hallingskeid   p. 199

Hallingskeid \'hä-liŋ-,sh^{y}aēd\ is a railroad station on the Bergen line, between Finse and Myrdal, on the Hardanger Plateau. There are many short tunnels and snow shelters between Finse and Myrdal; west of Myrdal the line passes through the Gravahals Tunnel, which is almost three miles (5 km) long. This part of the line joins the eastern and western parts of the country, which have distinct landscapes and even different traditional styles of building construction.

Reinunga \'raēn-,ùŋ-ä\ is the name of a valley, a lake, and

a tunnel just east of Myrdal station. Såta \'sȯ-tä\ is a mountain in the same area.

Sneoverbygget, "snow shelter": a roofed structure, partly open on the downhill side, built over railway tracks that run along a slope where avalanches are likely to occur.

We Who Live near the Railway   *p. 215*

In accordance with Rolf Jacobsen's wishes, the present Norwegian text restores wording that appeared in editions earlier than the *Samlede dikt* of 1977.

The Dovre \'dəv-re\ Mountains are a region of high mountains that spans the boundaries of four counties. Dovre is a railroad station in the Valley of Gudbrandsdal, just south of Dombås on the line to Trondheim, about 125 miles (200 km) northwest of Hamar. (For Gudbrandsdalen \'gū̇d-bräns-,däl-ᵊn\, see the note to "In the Varald Forest.")

Fokkstu \'fȯk-,stū̇\ is the first railroad station north of Dombås; the bogs lie in the surrounding area. Hjerkinn \'yar-kin\ is the third railroad station north of Dombås. The dome is an elevated area north and east of the station; it marks the highest point on the old "King's Highway" over the Dovre Mountains.

For *boggi*, see the note to "Railroad Country."

Fasten Your Seatbelts —   *p. 221*

Italic face in the translation marks phrases that are in English in the original poem.

The Media Poem   *p. 227*

Lake Mjøsa \'myœ̄-sä\ is the large lake upon which Hamar is situated.

Look Up (N.B. N.B.)   *p. 233*

Ullernåsen \'u̇l-ern-,ȯs-ᵊn\ is an affluent suburb west of Oslo.

Beyond Grorud — *p. 243*

Olav H. Hauge, a contemporary of Jacobsen, is considered one of the great Norwegian poets of this century.

Grorud \'grü-,rū̄d\ is a "satellite town" east of Oslo. Hakadal \'hä-kä-,däl\ is a town and railroad station about 12 miles (20 km) north of Oslo. Sokna \'sȯk-nä\ is a town and railroad station on the Bergen Line, about 40 miles (60 km) northwest of Oslo.

Hundvåko *p. 245*

Hundvåko \'hȯn-,vȯ-kü\, Hangur \'häŋ-,ūr\.

Skriulaupen \'skrē-yü-,laủʸp-ᵊn\, Framrusthovdi \'främrủst-,hȯv-dē\, and Uppnostindann' \'ủp-nȯs-,tin-dan/ are all mountains in Oppland.

Tindulvstølane \'tin-dủl-,stȫ-lä-ne\.

—More Mountains *p. 249*

Norway has had three kings named Harald \'hä-räl\. The sense of the poem suggests that "King Harald" here means Harald Hårfagre (the Fairhaired), whom tradition credits with having founded a united Norway in 872 A.D.

The Bells from Assisi *p. 253*

Assisi stands on a high plateau; when birds fly out from it they are immediately far above the surrounding plains. So "high against the heavens" is a precise image.

"Silvery Moon" *p. 255*

Italic face in the translation marks phrases that are in English in the original poem.

Kersey Coates is a section of Jackson, which is the part of Kansas City, Mo., that lies immediately to the southeast of the juncture of the two rivers.

The phrase *full og fager* at the end of the poem corresponds to "full and fair," but contains a pun, since *full* also means "drunk."

The Inland Line   p. 259

The Inland Line is the name of the entire rail line that runs down the center of Sweden from Gällivare in the north to Kristinehamn in the south (a distance of 780 miles or 1,290 km). The poem traces a trip south to Östersund. (North of Gällivare a connecting line continues to Narvik, on the northwest coast of Norway.)

The state built the part of the line that was hardest to build (from Gällivare to Steg, 575 miles or 930 km) between 1907 and 1937. The more southerly stretches were built much earlier in various stages by private companies and later taken over by the state. The main purpose of these early roads was to carry ore. By the turn of the century, however, the Swedish General Staff had realized that an extended and unified railway in the area would contribute significantly to the defense of northern Sweden. But the Inland Line did not prosper as was hoped.

Gällivare \'ye-li-,vä-re\ lies only four miles (6 km) south of Malmberget ("Ore Mountain"). It has been a center for mining in the area since the 1870s. Östersund \'œs-ter-,sund\, a city in central Sweden, was founded in the 1780s, developed slowly, and had only 500 inhabitants by 1850. The railroad arrived in 1882. In 1893 the Norrlands Artillery Regiment was garrisoned there; it was joined within twenty years by two other regiments.

Kåbdalis \'kob-,dä-lis\, Moskosel \'mus-ku-,sel\, Koosa-kåbbå \'kü-sä-'ko-bo\, also spelled Kuosakåbbå, and Varg-tandberget \'väry-,tän-'bar-yet\, also called Järvtandberget, are railroad stations on the line heading south from Gällivare. The poem's prophecy has been fulfilled: the last-named station is no longer on the map.

Vojmån \'voi-mon\ is a railroad station two-thirds of the way from Gällivare to Östersund. The Lule \'lü-le\, the Pite \'pē-te\, and the Ume \'ü-me\ are three large rivers in northern Sweden that flow from northwest to southeast across the entire breadth of the country and empty into the Gulf of Bothnia.

Ulriksfors \'ul-riks-,fosh\ is a town and railroad station about 55 miles (90 km) northeast of Östersund.

Bibliography: Books by Rolf Jacobsen

IN NORWEGIAN

Jord og jern. Oslo: Gyldendal, 1933.
Vrimmel. Oslo: Gyldendal, 1935.
Fjerntog. Oslo: Gyldendal, 1951.
Hemmelig liv. Oslo: Gyldendal, 1954.
Sommeren i gresset. Oslo: Gyldendal, 1956.
Brev til lyset. Oslo: Gyldendal, 1960.
Stillheten efterpå ———. Oslo: Gyldendal, 1960.
Dikt i utvalg. Ed. Asbjørn Aarnes and Emil Boyson. Oslo: Gyldendal, 1967.
Headlines. Oslo: Gyldendal, 1969.
Pass for dørene —dørene lukkes. Oslo: Gyldendal, 1972.
Samlede dikt. Oslo: Gyldendal (Lanterne), 1973.
Pusteøvelse. Oslo: Gyldendal, 1975.
Den ensomme veranda og andre dikt. Selected by the author. Oslo: Den norske Bokklubben, 1977.
Samlede dikt. Oslo: Gyldendal, 1977.
Tenk på noe annet. Oslo: Gyldendal, 1979.
Samlede dikt. Oslo: Gyldendal, 1982.

IN ENGLISH

Twenty Poems. Trans. Robert Bly. Madison, Minnesota: Seventies Press, 1977.
Breathing Exercise: Poems of Rolf Jacobsen. Trans. Olav Grinde. Buffalo, N.Y.: White Pine Press, 1985.

IN HUNGARIAN

A város metafizikája. Trans. Vince Sulyok. Budapest: Európa Könyvkiadó, 1978.

IN SWEDISH

Jord och järn. Trans. Christer Eriksson. Stockholm: Rabén & Sjögren, 1979.

IN DANISH
Deadline Kl. 23. Trans. Hans Reusch. Åbenrå: Prometheus, 1980.

IN RUSSIAN
Избранная лирика [Selected Poems]. Ed. L. Gorlina, trans. Yuri Vronsky. Moscow: Molodiya Gvardiya, 1982.

IN BULGARIAN
Кобалтово синьо [Cobalt]. Ed. Vera Gancheva. Sofia: Narodna Kultura, 1982.

Index to Norwegian Titles

ROLF JACOBSEN is one of Norway's most highly respected poets. He is a member of the Norwegian Academy of Language and Literature. Among the awards he has received are the Norwegian Critics' Prize (1960) and the Doubloug Prize of the Swedish Academy (1968). He has published eleven books—not counting collections—since his debut in 1933; his poetry has been translated into some twenty languages.

ROGER GREENWALD is a poet from New York who now lives in Toronto, where he teaches writing at Innis College in the University of Toronto. His poems and translations have appeared in *The World, Panjandrum, Poetry East, Scandinavian Review, Translation, The Spirit That Moves Us, Alcatraz, Rubicon* and *Stand*; and in WRIT magazine, which he founded in 1970 and continues to edit.

POUL BORUM, Danish poet and critic, has published numerous volumes of poetry and criticism since 1962; his poems have appeared in translation in many British and American magazines and anthologies. In English he has written *Danish Literature: A Short Critical Survey* (1979). In *Poetisk Modernisme* (1968), a critical introduction to European and American poetry from Baudelaire to the present, he was the first critic outside Norway to appreciate Rolf Jacobsen and place him in an international context.

The Lockert Library of Poetry in Translation

George Seferis: Collected Poems (1924-1955), translated, edited, and introduced by Edmund Keeley and Philip Sherrard. (Greece)

Collected Poems of Lucio Piccolo, translated and edited by Brian Swann and Ruth Feldman. (Italy)

C. P. Cavafy: Collected Poems, translated by Edmund Keeley and Philip Sherrard and edited by George Savidis. (Greece)

Benny Andersen: Selected Poems, translated by Alexander Taylor. (Denmark)

Selected Poetry of Andrea Zanzotto, translated and edited by Ruth Feldman and Brian Swann. (Italy)

Poems of René Char, translated by Mary Ann Caws and Jonathan Griffin. (France)

Selected Poems of Tudor Arghezi, translated and edited by Michael Impey and Brian Swann. (Romania)

"The Survivor," and Other Poems, by Tadeusz Różewicz, translated and introduced by Magnus J. Krynski and Robert A. Maguire. (Poland)

"Harsh World" and Other Poems, by Ángel Gonźalez, translated by Donald D. Walsh. (Latin America)

Ritsos in Parentheses, translations and introduction by Edmund Keeley. (Greece)

Salamander: Selected Poems of Robert Marteau, translated by Anne Winters. (France)

Angelos Sikelianos: Selected Poems, translated and introduced by Edmund Keeley and Philip Sherrard. (Greece)

Dante's Rime, translated by Patrick S. Diehl. (Italy)

Selected Later Poems of Marie Luise Kaschnitz, translated by Lisel Mueller. (Germany)

Osip Mandelstam's "Stone," translated by Robert Tracy. (Russia)

The Dawn Is Always New: Selected Poetry of Rocco Scotellaro, translated by Ruth Feldman and Brian Swann. (Italy)

Sounds, Feelings, Thoughts: Seventy Poems by Wisława Szymborska, translated by Magnus J. Krynski and Robert Maguire. (Poland)

The Man I Pretend to Be: "The Colloquies" and Selected Poems of Guido Gozzano, translated by Michael Palma with introduction by Eugenio Montale. (Italy)

D'Après Tout: Poems by Jean Follain, translated by Heather McHugh. (France)

Songs of Something Else: Selected Poems of Gunnar Ekelöf, translated by Leonard Nathan and James Larson. (Sweden)

The Little Treasury of One Hundred People, One Poem Each, compiled by Fujiwara No Sadaie and translated and annotated by Tom Galt. (Japan)

The Ellipse: Selected Poems of Leonardo Sinisgalli, translated by W. S. Di Piero. (Italy)

The Difficult Days by Roberto Sosa, translated by Jim Lindsey. (Honduras)

Hymns and Fragments by Friedrich Hölderlin, translated and introduced by Richard Sieburth. (Germany)

The Silence Afterwards: Selected Poems of Rolf Jacobsen, translated and edited by Roger Greenwald. (Norway)

Library of Congress Cataloging in Publication Data

Jacobsen, Rolf.
The silence afterwards.

(The Lockert library of poetry in translation)
"Bibliography: books by Rolf Jacobsen": p.
Includes index.
  1. Jacobsen, Rolf—Translations, English.
  I. Greenwald, Roger, 1945- . II. Title. III. Series.

PT8951.2.A38A24 1985   839.8'2172   85-42671
ISBN 0-691-06647-7   ISBN 0-691-01424-8 (pbk.)